IDL____

CW01911515

SLOW DOWN. HAVE FUN. LIVE WELL. JULY—AUGUST 2022

libertas per cultum

NO.85

IDLER NO.85 JULY–AUGUST 2022

Idler is a bi-monthly published by Idle Ltd.,
Great Western Studios, 65 Alfred Road, London W2 5EU   Tel: 0203 176 7907   idler.co.uk
Subscription enquiries: 01442 820 580 *or* contact@webscribe.co.uk

Editor: Tom Hodgkinson
Art Director: Alice Smith
Sub-editors: Michael Meekin
                      Cathi Unsworth
Typesetter: Christian Brett, Bracketpress
Programming Director: Victoria Hull
Festival Manager: Cathleen Mair
Poetry Editor: Clare Pollard
Editorial Assistant: Julia Lasica
Publishing Advisor: James Pembroke

Advertising: renata@parkwalkmedia.com

Printed and bound in the UK by Mixam

ISSN 1351-5098
ISBN 978-1-7396608-0-2

Cover illustration by Ellie Foreman-Peck
elliefp.co.uk

Editorial illustrations throughout
the *Idler* (except where noted)
by Alice Smith
alice-smith.co.uk

Contributors: Paul Shadbolt, Jon Link,
Mick Bunnage, Royston Robertson, Gray
Jolliffe, Arthur Smith, Hugo Deadman,
Mark Vernon, Alex Johnson, Marie-Louise
Plum, Kate Rew, Tara Bergin, Georgina
Williams, Annabel Sampson, Charlotte
Brook, Lee Osborne, Tim Richardson,
Rob Greer, Julia Lasica, Will Hodgkinson,
Stewart Lee, Peter Fincham, Graham
Burnett, Bill Anderson, Richard Hammond,
Lindsey Bareham, Oli Meade, Cameron
Murray, Joseph Piercy, Rachel Kelly,
Dominic Frisby, Virginia Ironside,
Alex Bellos

Letter from the Editor

Dear Idlers

"Be like water" said Lao Tzu. Water flows, fills empty vessels and will give way when you plunge into it but is so strong that it can dissolve solid elements. In this issue we celebrate watery things with reflections on gentle swimming from Kate Rew, an introduction to mudlarking from Marie-Louise Plum, tales from the philosopher Heraclitus from Mark Vernon, and a paddleboarding guide from green travel expert Richard Hammond.

Dr Johnson, it appears, was a fan of wild swimming and went sea-bathing in Brighton in 1769 and 1766. On the latter occasion, he got chatting with a "dipper" – a sort of lifeguard who dipped people into the sea. Johnson was in his late fifties but impressed the dipper with his swimming prowess. "Why Sir," said the dipper, "you must have been a stout-hearted gentleman forty years ago." On another occasion, said one biographer, he recklessly leapt into the river at Oxford and "swam away to a part of it that had been told of a as dangerous place."

Elsewhere, Bryan Ferry's new *Lyrics* book stirs up memories of early Roxy Music for Will Hodgkinson and Tim Richardson delves into the work of the great Heath Robinson.

Our cover star Jarvis Cocker is man who appears to go with the flow and certainly takes his time. For this issue I went to see him at The Gallery of Everything which was showing an exhibition of the ephemera which inspired his memoir, *Good Pop, Bad Pop*. And more than a memoir, the book could be read as a handbook for creative people, as you will discover in our interview. It's Jarvis's belief that we're all artists and I'm sure you'll find our chat to be inspiring as well as entertaining.

Live well,

Tom 👁

3

Contents

READER OFFERS…

Page 11 Buy a subscription: get a free book
Page 19 Online course: *The Idler Guide to Investing*
Page 155 Check out the Idler Academy's online courses

NOTES FROM
THE COUCH

Idler's Diary

The world seen through **Tom Hodgkinson's** *screen.*
Send your stories to us at mail@idler.co.uk

Pop Idle

Our cover star Jarvis Cocker headlines the third Idler Festival at Fenton House, 8–10 July. He'll be discussing his memoir *Good Pop, Bad Pop*. Is he an idler? Well, as you'll read on page 28, he is something of a slow worker. He conceived the idea for Pulp in 1978 when he was 15, but it wasn't until 1995 that Pulp finally made it big with the release of *Different Class*. A few years later, in 2001, the exhausted band took ten years off.

Only Disconnect

In 2017 France announced the "right to disconnect". The idea is to stop staff checking and sending work-related emails during their periods of leisure. Italy and Spain have followed suit, and Portugal has introduced a law that forbids companies from contacting employees outside working hours. Belgium has recently given this right to its civil servants. "It's when you're tempted to send an email because you finally have five minutes over the weekend to answer something you got on Friday," says Bruno Mettling, the former head of human resources at telecoms group Orange, who helped shape the 2017

law. "You need an alarm bell to go off in your head saying, 'You're only going to bother your colleague – it can wait.'"

American Nightmare

In the old days, the capitalists were fat, smoked cigars and wore top hats. These days, the men who make millions out of the toil of low-paid workers have managed to convince themselves they're reincarnations of Gandhi. One such is Howard Schultz, founder of the $140 billion Starbucks chain, purveyor of disgusting over-priced coffee in bland surroundings. At a gathering of Starbucks executives at the Buffalo Hyatt Regency in November 2021, he likened their tawdry business to a mental health charity. Noting that there is an epidemic of loneliness in the West, he said: "What company is going to be a better remedy for isolation and loneliness?" Even more unbelievably, some of the absurdly wealthy executives in the audience started to cry, so moved were they by the Christ-like altruism of their boss, according to an essay in *The Baffler* magazine. Is this the same Howard Schultz, asks the *Baffler*, who retains 30 lawyers from union-busting firm Littler Mendelson to "hamper and disrupt" unionisation drives among employees? (From Littler's website: "Littler understands the mindset of union organisers and stands ready to advise employers facing such tactics. Our deep experience in representing management serves as a strong counterpoint to the world's most powerful labour organisations. We guide companies in developing and initiating strategies that lawfully avoid unions or effectively respond to unconventional corporate campaigns.") Or the same Starbucks which sent staff out to local branches to tell workers that if they

*"It's so great to finally be able to
do normal things again."*

joined the Workers United union, they'd lose their free Spotify subscription?

Last of the Mohicans
Thanks to Czech reader and lifelong punk Vitek Formanek for sending us his new book, *68 Tunes of Punk*, a compilation of 68 interviews with punk bands old and new. Punk is important to many Czechs as a breath of freedom in contrast to the stifling authoritarianism of the communist period. Whenever there is a punk festival in Czecho, Vitek will be there with his partner Eva. Thus it is that he has met representatives of The Damned, Oi Polloi, The Adicts, Angel City Outcasts, Anti Pasti, Cock Sparrer, Dead Kennedys, Discharge, Eddie and the Hot Rods, The Exploited, GBH, The Lurkers, Peter and the Test Tube Babies, Subhumans, Subway Sect, The Vibrators, Vice Squad and UK Subs, all of whom are still touring despite being in their 60s and 70s.

Hard Times
In Northern Europe we all feel quite smug about the fact that chimney sweeps are no more and that children no longer lose their lives (or fingers) in the dark satanic mills of the early 19th century. However, according to the International Labour Organisation, 160 million children – almost one in ten worldwide – are still in child labour. Child labour, says the ILO, has grown particularly in the five to 11-year-old age group. One such

9

child was Domboué Nibéissé from Burkina Faso, who is now 15 years old. "When I was nine years old I had to leave school to work in the cotton fields," he told the ILO. "It was difficult work and tiring. We picked cotton by hand. There were a few other children working alongside me. I used to start sowing at 9am, rest around 1pm, and at 4pm I would go home. I was given between 500 and 700 francs [$0.79 to $1.19]."

When Domboué was 11, a school reintegration programme got him back into a sort of catch-up centre. "I learned to count and read in Dioula, we did our homework in Dioula, and then we learned to count and do calculations and homework in French. Thanks to this, I was able to go back to school in the formal system, in CM1 class [fourth year of primary school]." Director-General of the ILO, Guy Ryder, said: "Some may say that child labour is an inevitable consequence of poverty and that we have to accept that. But this is wrong. We can never resign ourselves to child labour. We do not have to. Tackling the root causes such as household poverty is essential. But make no mistake, child labour is a violation of a basic human right, and our goal must be that every child, everywhere is free from it. We cannot rest until that happens."

Dream On

"We now have time to dream," said lottery winners Joe and Jess Thwaite, celebrating their £184 million win in May. We're glad they're going to quit their jobs and plan to put their new-found free time to good use. However, we can't help but reflect that you really don't need to win £184 million in order to create the time to dream. That can be done right here, right now. We also predict with some confidence that the £184 million is very unlikely to help give the Thwaites time to dream, and will in fact present them with a non-stop nightmare as family members, charities, freeloaders, desperadoes and beggars of all stripes appear, competing for a slice of the fortune. 🔊

Arthur Smith
A Lesson in Mayhem

*Arthur Smith recalls a teacher's inspired
moment of madness in a PE lesson*

WHEN I WAS 20, I spent a year as a teaching assistant at a school in Paris and I liked to wind my pupils up some mornings by writing something provocative on the blackboard as soon as I arrived. When I scrawled, "English food is the best in the world," I learnt that the French word for "eurgh!" is *"beark!"*. English food, they informed me, is disgusting (*"dégueulasse"*). We put jam on meat and we like baked (pronounced to rhyme with "smackhead") beans. We are also inveterate gobblers of *"la gêlée,"* by which they meant fruit jelly, a dish abhorrent and comical to any right-thinking Parisian.

Feeling an obligation to my nationality, I determined to defend jelly and, since it was unavailable in France, persuaded my mother to send me some packets, which I prepared and took to school. My pupils were unanimous in their contempt for English jelly. My pedagogic initiative earned me only a telling-off from the school cleaner and a messy hour spent scraping the morsels of wobbly phosphorescence from the walls of the classroom.

Are you a teacher? Then this article is dedicated to you. I've always felt a connection between teaching and stand-up comedy. In both you have to hold the attention of a crowd of disparate people for an hour – but as a teacher you have to do six or seven shows a day. And teachers aren't allowed to swear.

Of all the lessons I had as a child, one stands out as the most entertaining and instructive session in all my schooldays. It was in my final term at primary school, and it involved Mrs Logan, who took PE in the school hall on the first floor. We didn't have any special kit, but for some reason we boys were required to remove our shorts, with their stains and comforting marbles, and do the exercises in our underpants. By the age of 11, this had become extremely embarrassing. We felt sheepish and vulnerable in front of the girls, who had no such humiliating requirement.

As we gingerly stripped off one

culture war
can I use your lavatory?
we call it the shitter in this house, now fucking get out

day, Tom Simpson got his shorts caught on the end of his foot and kicked them free with such alacrity that they sailed through the air, straight out of an open window and down to the playground below.

There was a moment while everyone took in this stupendous occurrence. Then, of course, came shrieks of laughter. Tom Simpson, stricken with shame, began to cry as all the embarrassment we other boys felt suddenly rushed from us to him. The girls were laughing hard too. Everyone, except Mrs Logan and Simpson, was shrieking with the fun of it. Poor old Tom.

Eventually Mrs Logan regained an uneasy silence but not control. The lesson was in disarray until, in a moment of inspiration she surely never surpassed in her teaching career, Mrs Logan shouted. "Right! All you boys, throw your shorts out the window!"

What a fantastic invitation! Tom's emasculation was forgotten; he stopped sobbing as we queued up to launch our shorts through the window. The occasion had become funny in a good way such that even Mrs Logan and Tom were enjoying themselves. In fact, Tom now looked like a trail-blazing hero. The children in the class below must also have relished the strange sight of the sky raining boys' shorts. As we trouped down to retrieve them, chortling and tittering, our new-found solidarity meant that the giggling girls now seemed admiring rather than threatening, and I learnt the truth that one man in his pants in public is pitiable, but ten is a posse of fun.

I wonder if anyone else who was there that day remembers this incident. Tom Simpson might, and possibly Mrs Logan too, if she's still alive, but I doubt anyone else does. The images of youth that stay with us into adulthood often seem to others arbitrary and without apparent significance. Or maybe it was for others in the class the astounding event that lives in my mind. At any rate, ever since that PE lesson the phrase has periodically returned to me, acting as a call to arms, a bold plan in a tricky situation, an invitation to creative mayhem. Boys, throw your shorts out the window. ◉

How I Live
Hugo Deadman, priest

As a speechwriter to the wealthy and powerful, Hugo's life was a million miles from the Church. Until a Pauline moment made him change the script

IT IS 1988. I am at Peterborough United football ground for an anarchist festival. I am on stage, the singer in a punk band, Chopper, supporting a better-known punk band called Chaos UK. Tom, now *Idler* editor, is on bass, and contributor James on drums. I am pencil-thin, with a shock of peroxide hair. I am shouting the chorus of our show-stopping, if brief, anthem: "We're So Skinny, You're So Fat". An anarchist from Peterborough has taken umbrage, leapt on stage and punched me. As I fall, I think: "I've bitten off more than I can chew."

Now it is 2019 at Portsmouth Cathedral. Alas, I have no hair to speak of. There is considerably more of me, so I am in no position to sing that chorus. I am leaning against a wall and throwing up = because I'm just about to be ordained as a clergyman. Once again, I'm thinking, "I've bitten off

Chopper – with Hugo leaning forward and wearing Watchman t-shirt

more than I can chew. I'm not up to it. I'm a fraud."

I still think that every day. I'm a priest in Portsmouth, in the sort of old-school, working class community my grandparents came from: resourceful, resilient and remarkable. Like most jobs there is structure, graft and frustration. I'm in church at 8.30 to say prayers on behalf of the whole community. We pray for every street in the parish every month. We pray for people who have been asked to be prayed for – and for people we know who are sick. And we ring the bell to let people know that's what we're about. There was genuine grief in lockdown when people didn't hear the bell. People lost a pulse and a comfort in their day.

Days often involve putting together labyrinthine liturgies, a great deal of admin, wrestling with photocopiers, dealing with suppliers – all the grit of working life, but it does get in your eyes. There's also a great deal of pastoral stuff; calling people, taking communion to them at home – and especially at Christmas and Easter, huge numbers of school assemblies. I did 14 in the fortnight before Easter.

Food is a big issue in ministry; it's a very cake-heavy environment. Lunch is usually a cheese and Marmite toastie at Milton Perk, run by the excellent Shaun. I spend a lot of time sitting in cafés. You get known. People see someone with a collar and want to talk, often to unload. Then it's back to church at 5.30 for more prayers.

Sundays are full on; mass at eight, again at ten, then often a baptism or two – and then night prayers at 8pm. It's always great. But it does leave me whacked.

My one great indulgence is football. Fratton Park is in the parish. The challenge is to remember you're wearing a collar at the match. My language has occasionally not been from the *Book of Common Prayer*.

So every day is full of ordinary stuff. But every day is also full of big stuff and I have no idea what I'm doing. I do know this, though: my job is to get alongside people and love them, often people it's hard to love.

So the highs touch the sky. Someone unburdens themselves about childhood grief, walking away visibly lighter. A grieving daughter says you've helped her to hope again. You baptise 74-year-old Barry. The whole of Milton Park Primary want to fist-bump you because they enjoyed your assembly. ("Let's shout Hosanna like the crowd in Jerusalem! I can't hear you! Louder!")

The lows are deep and black. Holding the hand of a 48-year-old in a hospice. A month ago you were exchanging texts about football. Now you both know he has 24 hours left. Or a pauper's funeral. It's only you there. On days like that, I don't pray. I shout and shake my fist at the sky.

But the first of those paupers' funerals – for Arlene Ayling – also showed me something very big does indeed remain. That I had to stand in for everyone she'd met. As she left I was there to say her life mattered, it had significance.

Oddly, my decade as a political speechwriter is grist to that mill. It also led to me getting out. I'd run a Cabinet Committee, been a minister's private secretary, written for two Justice Secretaries – then gone into the City to write for the Lord Mayor, then the CEO of a FTSE100 company. I was sitting in the latter's office as he recounted his endless triumphs as Master of the Universe – and I realised how bent out of shape I was. How I'd let my mouth be stuffed with gold and I couldn't breathe. I was helping people, who already felt they were lords of all, to feel imperial. I didn't care about them. But I knew what I did care about and what I was called to.

Speechwriting was all about how individual stories tell a bigger story. So is ministry. Our church is a standard red brick gothic box. I know the story of everything in it, who gave it, why, what it signifies. I keep and tell those stories – and try to show how they are entwined with and part of the humongous, resonant, reverberating Christian story.

I hope I'm the opposite type of leader to the people I used to work for. The people I serve teach and lead me. I reflect back their teaching, virtue and value. I came back to faith in Hackney because I saw God in the eyes of the poor. I see the same thing expressed differently in Portsmouth. The truth of the Gospel is in their lives. It's deeply moving to witness.

It's also deeply political. We give a voice to the voiceless. We build a community as a church – and that community is the foundation of a new Jerusalem, built from the bottom up, from the densely packed terraced streets of PO4. There are no glittering temples or palaces. It is nonetheless the City of God. ◉

Philosophy

The Flux of the Matter

Everything is in a state of flux, as Heraclitus's maxim goes.
But do the ancient philosopher's words point towards a deeper meaning?
asks **Mark Vernon**

ONE OF THE best-known comments in Western philosophy has to do with rivers. The flowing thought was uttered by the ancient Ephesian hermit Heraclitus. Born into a patrician family during the sixth century BC, he despaired of the way human beings conduct themselves and so sought hope in the nonhuman vitalities around him. Watercourses must have been a favourite fount of inspiration.

"You would not step twice into the same river." This is how Plato records the famous aphorism – the word "aphorism" being derived from the same root as "horizon": an aphorism invites you to peer over the horizon of your current perceptions and detect more.

The common way of interpreting Heraclitus's remark is to take it as illustrating one of his central doctrines: everything is in a state of flux. "In the same river, ever different waters flow," is the way he puts it in another saying that survives.

But notice a detail that I think is key. The river is the same. It changes with the waters that move through it, but contains those waters within its unchanging banks. A deeper perception of reality is on Heraclitus's mind, which, if glimpsed, reveals something less ordinary. The psychiatrist and philosopher Iain McGilchrist is one of the best modern exponents of what Heraclitus invites us to contemplate. The ancient Greek did not stop at flow and flux, McGilchrist suggests. His deeper fascination was the coincidence of seeming opposites. In the case of the river, the opposites are the coming together of its firm banks and running waters. The two apparently contrary dynamics make the one sparkling entity.

In his latest book, *The Matter With Things*, McGilchrist argues that nothing less than the flourishing of Western civilisation depends upon relearning the ability to hold superficially irreconcilable differences in creative tension. He maintains that the modern world is plagued by the tendency to see things in only one way. Nature is a machine, not an organism: power is about exercising control, not offering gifts; progress and growth must govern decisions, not the pursuit of joy and transcendence. Our culture has rocketing abilities to manipulate the world and a fast-fading ability to find any meaning in it. Life has become a zero-sum game. The winner takes it all.

Heraclitus calls across the millennia, saying: consider again the nature of the river. Ask it to disclose more of reality. Its rushing water and steady verges come to our aid. What is revealed, McGilchrist explains, is that "all is neither simply single, nor simply manifold, neither simply whole, nor simply not whole, neither simply like nor simply unalike, each thing working with, and by the same token working against, the others; that the One and the Many bring one another forth into being."

What look like contraries can be seen to collaborate and the world shows itself to be structured not by rigid rules or enemies in conflict; that view is a dangerous delusion and murderous falsehood. Rather, life flows through cycles, held in polarities that are distinctive but not ultimately different, like the two ends of the one magnet. The mountain needs the valley. The

skin separates and connects. The bird resists the air and so soars in it.

The awareness of such a moving, vibrant harmony brings an unexpected benefit. We can both remain a part of what's going on around us, and stand back from the turbulence or delight, to discover a peace which passes understanding: a state of undefended engagement with existence that is composed

though not detached, and so is capable of facing anything life or death might bring. The experience of living is transformed not because the inner calm separates itself from whatever is happening, but for precisely the opposite reason. What's truly steady can embrace what's gleefully transient, which means that the dark and the light can be accepted. The consumptive approach to surviving – "I want this, I don't want that" – falls away, along with the anxiety, fear and dread.

Social and political ramifications follow, as well. Take modern science. People are inclined to treat the scientific approach as equating enlightenment with empirical proof and solid evidence. But if everything that comes our way is forced through the sieve of statistics and testing, whatever the science doesn't detect will be ignored, if not actively discarded. A scientific civilisation is, therefore, at risk of relying on its powers of prediction and so tripping up when the unexpected happens; it believes it has the ability to understand everything, given big enough budgets and fast enough computers, though grows increasingly endarkened as the subtler pulses and gentler spirits of the human psyche and world soul are ignored. What cannot be calculated cannot be comprehended, what cannot be modelled cannot be embraced, what cannot be measured cannot

be understood, what cannot be manipulated cannot be brought into life-giving relation.

The river tells us more. It murmurs a warning about artificial intelligence, which is dangerous not only because AI narrows our take on life, but because AI strives to remake the world according to the parameters it deploys. The river adds a hope – that facing tension can lead to a realisation that hate is transcended by love. The river continues with a thought on how letting go is lovelier than holding onto. The river even asks us to consider that our last breath may be the necessary exhalation before awakening to another mode of existence.

Little wonder that rivers are often thought to be personalities. In some countries, the personhood of mighty watercourses is being recognised by the awarding of legal rights, as if the flows of water are people. I think Heraclitus knew that rivers were not people but they are principles, powers and presences with their own characteristics and message.

They bring and they carry away. They manifest as trickles and inundations. They connect the source to the winding delta, which then merges with the unimaginable expanse of the sea. "We step and do not step into the same rivers, we are and we are not," Heraclitus also mused. Such is the genius of life. ☉

Idler Heroes
Escape Rooms

Is there a more idler-friendly way to write than while reclining on a hotel bed and enjoying a sip of sherry? Alex Johnson *salutes the* modus operandi *of a literary giant*

NATURALLY I ADMIRE Maya Angelou for her creative output, her dedication to the craft of writing, and her inspiring approach to speaking out on social wrongs. But what I also respect about the author of *I Know Why the Caged Bird Sings* is the soothing atmosphere she created in which to write.

During the lockdowns, a lot of people discovered that what they really needed was a distinct space in which to work. Or as Virginia Woolf famously put it in a lecture in 1929, "a room of one's own". For writers, somewhere private, quietish, and comfortable is particularly important, somewhere to get away from the distractions of home life when settling down to put pen to paper. And what more comfortable way of doing so is there than to check into a hotel?

The list of hotel-based writers is impressively long. Ernest Hemingway found the surroundings of room 551 in the Hotel Ambos Mundos in Havana sufficiently inspiring to write parts of *For Whom The Bell Tolls* and *Death in the Afternoon* (the room has since become a tiny museum in his honour). As The Savoy hotel in London's writer-in-residence in 2002, Fay Weldon was given a £350-a-night room for three months to write for whichever projects she pleased. And a veritable Who's Who of scribblers chose the Chelsea Hotel in New York, including Jack Kerouac, William Burroughs, and Arthur C Clarke, who produced the screenplay for *2001: A Space Odyssey* in room 1008.

But arguably the most dedicated hotel writer was Maya Angelou (1928–2014). Her working routine was to wake early and head to a pleasant but unremarkable hotel room near her home, which she rented by the month. She deliberately chose fairly spartan surroundings, small rooms with nothing more than a bed and perhaps a basin, and with the hotel art works on the walls removed – "We need much less than we think we need," she once said.

The only things she brought with her from home were a bottle of sherry for occasional nips (usually at elevenses but sometimes earlier depending on mood, a habit she dropped later in life), a deck of cards, a copy of the King James Bible, and a dictionary, sometimes a Thesaurus and crossword puzzles.

Work started around 6.30am–7am once she had connected with her working environment and put the outside world out of her head. "It's lonely," she said, "and it's marvellous."

Illustration by James Oses

Angelou kept the identity of these hotels a secret and admitted that she relied upon loyal hotel staff to keep interruptions to a minimum (though they did come in to empty the wastebasket and after a few weeks attempt to change the sheets) and feign ignorance when people asked if she were in the building. Her home in later years was Winston-Salem in North Carolina and it's likely that the city's Historic Brookstown Inn and Kimpton Cardinal Hotel were among her chosen writing locations.

In her hotel room, she would lie down on the bed to write entirely in longhand on yellow legal pads, thus also joining that happy bunch of writers who found vertical writing far too arduous – Truman Capote once described himself as a "completely horizontal author" and like Angelou was also partial to a sherry or two during the writing day.

Quite content with producing about a dozen pages a day, she then returned home around lunchtime and very sensibly took a break from writing until later in the evening, deliberately putting it all out of her mind to concentrate on getting dinner ready. "I'm not totally absorbed in my work," she acknowledged in a 1983 interview. Indeed, while she was no slacker, she had an admirably idlerish approach to life. "Don't make money your goal," she said. "Instead pursue the things you love doing." Or as she puts it in her poem "When I Think About Myself":

My life has been one great big joke,
A dance that's walked,
A song that's spoke

Angelou was a keen and much-admired cook, and indeed wrote a couple of popular cookbooks: *Hallelujah! The Welcome Table*, a kind of food-based autobiography featuring mostly recipes inherited from her grandmother and mother, and the marvellously titled *Great Food, All Day Long: Cook Splendidly, Eat Smart*.

After dinner with her husband, she would sometimes read him what she'd written that day, or do a little light editing on her typewriter, the kind of Oxford Hours schedule as outlined in an Idler blog by management philosopher Charles Handy (idler.co.uk/article/goodbye-nine-to-five-hello-oxford-hours). It all sounds highly civilised.

Alex Johnson is the author of Rooms of Their Own: Where Great Writers Write, *illustrated by James Oses, (Frances Lincoln, £19.99)*

IDLER

Advertise!

Put your product or service in front of a like-minded audience of discerning mavericks who are time-rich, mature and with high disposable income

For a media pack with full reader profile and rates please contact renata@parkwalkmedia.com

FEATURES

Interview: Jarvis Cocker

Jarvis and the Machine

Tom Hodgkinson meets Jarvis Cocker at his Good Pop, Bad Pop exhibition to talk about Blu Tac, traffic cones, photocopiers and world domination. Photo opposite page: David Owens. All other photos: Dirk Lindner.

I<small>T'S A SUNNY AFTERNOON</small> in old London town. I'm at the Gallery of Everything to meet Jarvis Cocker. It's a small space in Marylebone dedicated to outsider and underground art. The gallery was formerly a barber's and retains its peeling flock wallpaper and tiled fireplaces. Directly opposite, enormous cars drop off tall blonde models in shades and strange-looking gentlemen with beards and long blond hair, wearing pink suits and espadrilles. It's the Chiltern Firehouse, a celebrity hangout.

Jarvis has chosen the gallery to host an exhibition of ephemera from his life – family photos, concert tickets, an old guitar, notebooks, vinyl records, books, a bit of Imperial Leather soap in a matchbox, Super 8 movies – many of which are featured in his book *Good Pop, Bad Pop*. I walk through the gallery, go downstairs, and find Jarvis in a small room at the back, fiddling with an old tape recorder. I ask him how the exhibition came to be.

The exhibition of the book: James Brett and Jarvis at The Gallery of Everything.
The show ran in May and June 2022

"The book is based on objects, so I thought it would be good to show them," he replies. "I've worked with [the gallery's owner] James Brett before. I like it here because it's not a normal gallery. It's not antiseptic – it's more like being in someone's house and I thought that was kind of appropriate."

The walls of the tiny room are covered in Pulp-related cuttings, gig posters and pages from Jarvis's teenage notebooks, where he sketched out his ideas for the band. There's also his In Tensai rhythm machine, Hopf electric guitar – given to him by his mum's Danish boyfriend – a moon landing toy, an old portable TV and a copy of *Record Mirror*.

"I wanted this to feel like my teenage bedroom," he says. "When I was putting stuff up on these walls, I regressed to being 15 again. It was that feeling of using Blu Tac: tearing bits off, putting a bit in each corner, and not wanting to waste it. It was such a weird thing, to go back into doing that, and worry about whether you were sticking it on straight."

"What do you have on your bedroom wall now?" I ask.

"Nothing. Wallpaper. Very tasteful wallpaper."

We look at black-and-white A4 posters with hand-drawn logos advertising early Pulp gigs.

"Photocopiers were the big enabler in those days."

Jarvis fiddles with the In Tensai – a cassette player with a built-in drum machine. Strange noises emerge. A looped three-note melody with noise in the background. Possibly reminiscent of the music on *Eraserhead* or similar.

"This is the first atonal rehearsal we did. It's almost recognisable as music. But it isn't music at all. I think we recorded some bits at the wrong speed."

Even at 16, then, Jarvis was experimenting madly. It's this collision of commercial pop and a love of the underground that makes him distinctly Jarvis.

"Let's have a wander round," he says.

Pulp-tastic: The Jarvis Bedroom Room ©Dirk Linder

Photo © Dirk Linder

Woodchip on the wall: Jarvis as a Boy

Tell Me When the Spaceship Lands

On the wall in the basement are lovely colour photos of Jarvis and his family members. We look at a picture of a jovial looking old man.

"That's my granddad. He took all these pictures. I found a box that said 'family' on it after he died. And these slides were inside. This is me and my sister in Torquay. I have to credit James Brett with getting these in. He liked them. None of these are in the book."

"Who's that with the beehive?"

"That's my Auntie Rita. And there's me with a purple shirt on and a tie."

He points to a pic of himself at around eight years old looking Pulp-like even then.

"You seem like a very jolly child in these photos. Did you have a basically happy childhood?"

"Yes, I think I did, and that's what I get from these pictures. My father left when I was seven and my mum's brother died around the same time. On paper that doesn't look so great. But I felt very secure – there was a lot of love in the family. It was a very female-dominated environment.

"Here's a rare photo of my father. I quite like this one because we're in a lunar module, like he's about to send us up into space. That was very shortly before he left. It was in the wake of the moon landing."

"What happened to your dad?"

"He left and went to Australia. He was a DJ there. He worked at the ABC – their equivalent of the BBC. And he was apparently quite well respected. Me and my sister did try and track him down but didn't find him."

There's a pile of black bin bags in the corner. I wonder why they haven't been cleared our. After all, the exhibition is open. Then I see the label: "Bin Bag Installation, Jarvis Cocker".

We walk to the converted coal cellar, where old film footage is showing.

"This is stuff from a TV programme called *Revolver* from 1978. It's the raw footage from the cameras so they're filming the audience and there are some amazing people there. Just kids messing about really. That's the thing about good pop. It brings the energy out of people."

We go upstairs. Jarvis unlocks a glass case and removes a tatty exercise book. This is where the 15-year-old Cocker outlined his plans for world domination.

"I'd forgotten I'd done this," he says.

There are pages and pages of his notes about the band subverting the record industry.

"I obviously took some trouble. But I ran out of ideas when I got to television."

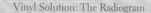

Vinyl Solution: The Radiogram

Photo ©Dirk Linder

Black Bin Liner installation and Super 8s. [below:] Jarvis's spaceship, keyboard and mini telly

"How much of it actually came true?" I wonder.

"Well, we got some stardom. I wrote here that we were going to have our own label which will turn into a radio station which will revolutionise the music business. I suppose we didn't actually manage that. But we had a go. And I'm glad I had ambitions to be something more than just famous. There was always going to be something subversive about it."

"The Pulp thing was that supposedly throwaway things would reveal something more profound. Throwaway items could tell you more than revered things. That formed the basic idea of Pulp. That's why it always had

to be pop songs. Would you like some chewing gum?" He offers me some Wrigley's Extra. A 1980s pack of it is an item in the book. But this is the modern version. "They've ruined it – look at the horrible logo now. I was horrified when they changed the label."

How to be Creative

Jarvis's book has a lovely tone. It's sardonic, self-effacing, warm, chatty, direct. He credits his editor for helping him to get the tone right…

"Part of the editing process was to read it out loud," he says. "It was during Covid so we were doing it by Zoom. [I would] read a page to my editor, Ana Fletcher. That really helped because if my sentence construction was a bit off, it was obvious. So it helped to get it to flow. Originally the loft stuff was going to be a small part of it, but Ana said that's the most interesting part, and I should make it all about that. I thought about it and realised she was right."

He's also got a nice way of directly addressing the reader, so you feel part of his life.

"I think that comes from doing the radio stuff. I do that quite a bit in [Radio 4 series] *Wireless Nights*. I say things like, 'Let's walk down here.' I quite like that – it makes it feel like you're in it together."

We talk about one of Jarvis's hobbyhorses, which is creativity. He believes that everyone is an artist.

"I do think everybody's got creative ability within them. It's whether you choose to try to develop it or not. You can make something from anything, as you can see from looking at this stuff."

I comment that the book is inspiring. Jarvis makes art look possible, achievable.

"It's not a self-help book but if it had that effect I'd be pretty pleased. I believe that everybody's got the ability to do it. At the end of our performance at Glastonbury, I did a speech saying, 'If a lanky git from Sheffield like me can get here, that means anybody could.' It's true. To me, that's the magic of the idea of pop. That's what makes good pop. Good pop is inclusive. Everybody can join in. If they want to. Sometimes it might pay off, and you would become a pop star. And that's exciting.

"I used to do a talk where we'd look at slides of traffic cones. Obviously a traffic cone is a thing for controlling traffic. But also, students might put them in their bedroom. Kraftwerk used to have traffic cones on the front of their early records. If you're a Krautrock fan, you might see a traffic cone and immediately think of Kraftwerk. Whereas someone else might think of when they were at university. You build up a web of references. You re-create the world depending on that latticework you've made for yourself. Does that make sense? And I think everybody is being an artist all the time. You might sometimes have a false assumption of a situation or of a person, based on the fact that you don't like their trousers. You're making those decisions all the time, often without even realising."

On Being Slow

One of the many charming elements of the book is Jarvis as slowcoach. It's a theme in his life. There's an amazing picture of young Pulp where Jarvis cradles a model tortoise.

"I wish I could be more productive," he says. "But that's one of the weird things in the book. I found this photograph where I'm holding a tortoise, as if it's a premonition of what life has in store for me."

He says he's come to terms with his low rate of productivity.

"There's no wrong or right way to do anything. I just have to accept that that's the way that works for me. Stuff has to be in there for a while and ferment. And then it turns into something."

How Jarvis Writes

The book was written over a number of years, partly at Jarvis's house in the Peak District, and partly in his Paris flat, which he visits in order to see his student age son who lives there.

"There was never a certain number of hours but I had specific places [to write in]. When I was in the Peak District, I had a garden table which I sat at. I had the view out of the window, if I wanted to look at the outside world. It was a very small room. No sound whatsoever. That would have distracted me. I wrote some of it in Paris, always with the window open behind me so I was aware of external reality, but it was all happening behind me. Always on a computer, never freehand. Sometimes on trains. I found trains a pleasant place to write."

The book's very visual.

"We had to get the design stuff right. I put pictures in the text as I was writing to refer to them. I'd been talking to [graphic designer] Julian House about books we like."

Jarvis shows me a 1969 copy of *The Medium is the Massage: An Inventory of Effects* by Marshall McLuhan and Quentin Fiore. The cover shows a girl wearing a pop art dress which reads LOVE. Inside are photos, collages, experimental typesetting. I remember this book lying around in my parents' house. Now, Jarvis's book doesn't look much like this one – but you can see how it's influenced the design.

"Mis-remembering," he says, "is often an important part of creativity."

Kick-Ass Cocker

While he may be lanky, Jarvis is not afraid to stand up for himself. There's a lovely scene in the book where he kicks a concert promoter up the arse.

"That was at Brunel University. They invaded the stage and tried to throw us off. It was in the heat of the moment. I'm not a violent person. It just seemed rude that they were doing that. Unfortunately you do have to defend yourself sometimes. You're the first person who's accused me of being an arse-kicker. Interesting."

And that reminded me of his famous mooning at Michael Jackson.

Bunnymen and Beatles

We go to the small room at the back and Jarvis shows me a copy of *Record Mirror* from the eighties, with Ian McCullough on the cover.

"It's funny. Maybe it's something to do with putting this show together, but I dreamt about Ian McCullough last night. It was really weird…he was wearing these ridiculously short shorts. And I said to him, 'You can't wear them, Ian.'"

Jarvis then plays another cassette of Pulp practising in the eighties. Electric guitars twang and there are muffled Northern voices.

"Sounds a bit like The Beatles rehearsing," I say.

"No. Definitely more basic than that. I realised early on that being like The Beatles was never going to happen. Just too musical. I had to set my sights lower."

Jarvis's First Song

The first song he wrote was called "Shakespeare Rock."

> "*Got a baby only one thing wrong*
> *She quote Shakespeare all day long*
> *I said baby, why you ignoring me?*
> *She said, 'To be or not to be.'*
> "Maybe I'll perform it at the Idler Festival." 😎

The Gallery of Everything, 4 Chiltern Street, London W1. ge@gallevery.com. Opening hours: Tue-Sat: 11–6.30pm, Sun: 2–6pm and by appointment. The Jarvis show has now closed but keep an eye on what they're up to. Jarvis Cocker's Good Pop, Bad Pop *(Allen Lane) is out now, £20*

Photo © Sheffield Star

Essay

Time and Tide

*Combining a love of history with the joy of discovery, and offering
the chance for contemplation while strolling through nature,
mudlarking could be the perfect idling pursuit.
Foreshore fan* **Marie-Louise Plum** *has the nitty gritty*

"Ever since man first quenched his thirst in its waters,
he has left his mark on the riverbed"
– Ivor Noël Hume, *Treasure in the Thames* (1956)

I'M A MODERN-DAY mudlark. The River Thames is my time machine. In
plucking a find from its foreshore, I'm probably the first person to touch
that object in hundreds, if not thousands, of years.

More likely than not you've heard of mudlarking, the name given to the
whimsical activity of searching a tidal riverbed, or foreshore, at low tide. It's
a pastime that has exploded in popularity over the last couple of years. The
number of licensed mudlarks in London currently stands at 3,800.

**Since I've been searching the Thames, my finds have
included silver coins, Georgian love tokens, mediaeval
pilgrim badges and Roman hypocaust tiles**

The term mudlark came into use at the end of the 18th century. It referred
to unfortunates – later described by the Victorian journalist and social reform
advocate Henry Mayhew as "poor creatures, most deplorable in appearance"
– who would scour the Thames for items of saleable value, such as "coals,
old-iron, rope, bones, copper nails".

These days mudlarking is a leisure pursuit, albeit one that's often taken
very seriously by its participants. Mudlarks search for lost, discarded, and
forgotten objects, washed up by chance for one tide only – tobacco pipes
thrown from the bear pits of Southwark, 17th-century trade tokens dropped
by tavern-going revellers.

Twice daily, from Teddington to the Thames Estuary, the river level rises
and falls by up to 24 feet. Searching this sunken channel seven metres below

Marie-Louise Plum
Photo by Tom Harrison

street level, I recover objects inextricably linked to London. The mud of the River Thames is free of oxygen, which means anything cocooned in it remains well preserved. The moment an object is dislodged from the riverbed, it begins to erode. Before this process happens, mudlarks aim to recover, preserve and record our finds, whether they're pieces of actual treasure or slices of social history.

New finds keep coming because the foreshore itself is eroding, with motorised river traffic and each tidal wash. So, clay pipes, the cigarette butts of their day, coins and other treasures will be around for some time to come.

In the six years I've been searching the Thames, I've found many historical items: Roman hypocaust tiles, Georgian love tokens and mediaeval pilgrim badges; silver coins showing portraits of those kings and queens who oversaw religious persecutions and the unification of nations; decorative glass beads, used in the trade and bartering of "human cargo", described by anthropologist Dr Anne Yentsch as "silent witnesses" of the past.

Members of the Order, whose motto was Lubrication in Moderation, would meet up to enjoy "beer, beef, and baccy", and were given titles such as Blaster, Tornado and Grand Typhoon

Every mudlark has their own specialist area of interest, be it coins, cufflinks or clay pipes. My fascination relates to something bigger than the object itself: the clues I glean from it. A maker's name and address on a Victorian button, for example. Such clues have led me to outrageous tales of larceny and looting in the expansive archives of the Old Bailey.

It was exhilarating to find a Spanish "pirate" coin, possibly dropped from the pocket of a swashbuckling sea dog returning from plundering a Spanish Armada ship. I was thrilled to discover a pierced silver coin, minted in the reign of James VI, given perhaps as a love token.

However, to find an everyday item with a tantalising hint of a clue that leads you to discover more about the real lives of real people – that's the exciting long-game of mudlarking: it's not just about facts and figures and immovable dates, but relatable histories we can imagine our own not-too-distant ancestors inhabiting.

A while ago, over two consecutive trips, I found a clay tobacco pipe and a silver cufflink, both directly linked to a little-known association with a wonderful story behind it. The Ancient Order of Froth Blowers was a humorous members' club whose name spoofed such haughtily titled organisations as the Royal Antediluvian Order of Buffaloes. Set up in 1924 by

40

14th–17th century silver hammered coins

ex-soldier Herbert Temple, the Froth Blowers' purpose was to raise £100 (equivalent to £5,600 today) for a children's charity founded Sir Alfred Fripp, a surgeon who had saved Temple's life.

Members of the Order, whose motto was Lubrication in Moderation, would meet up to enjoy "beer, beef, and baccy", and were given titles such as Blaster, Tornado and Grand Typhoon. The highest-ranking member, the "Senior Blower", would open meetings with the command "Gentlemen, shoot your linen", at which point everyone projected their shirt cuffs through their jacket sleeves to reveal official Ancient Order of Froth Blowers cufflinks.

Other titles given out were "Blowers" (men), "Fairy Belles" (women), and "Faithful Bow Wows" (children and dogs). The Order lasted until 1931, attracting 700,000 members and amassing a colossal £100,000 – nearly £6 million in today's money. The money was raised through membership fees and "fines" for such transgressions as not wearing cufflinks.

The chances of finding these related objects, directly one after the other, were slim, but it happened. There's magic in mudlarking. Or to put in the

20th century lead toy gun

words of my own motto: Don't be needy, don't be greedy; the finds will find you.

Although originating on the Thames, mudlarking can take place on any tidal river. I recently went searching on the Mersey Estuary and found nothing but rubble clearance and some WWII anti-tank defences. But then, just as I was about to call it a day, serendipity struck again. I looked down to see a rectangular block of sandstone, half a metre long, engraved with a skull and crossbones and three sets of initials: "TN", "LN" and "RN". I started thinking of adventure books I'd read as a child, stories of treasure chests and maps where X marked the spot.

Just as I was about to call it a day, serendipity struck again. I looked down to see a rectangular block of sandstone engraved with a skull and crossbones

I contacted the Coastal and Intertidal Zone Archaeological Network straightaway and they immediately visited the estuary to record the find. Sadly, no one was able to say for certain what the sandstone block was for, and the mystery remains to this day.

But this is another aspect to mudlarking: some finds have no answers, and

Georgian skeleton key

we must be content with that. Even so, there's plenty of fun to be had in investigating them. I once found a fragment of a Victorian/Edwardian roof tile inscribed "Made by FW Bol, Ponty P, Oct" and committed myself to searching every census return for the Pontypridd and Pontypool areas from the years 1890 to 1930. I didn't find any matches for the tile-maker's name but it's not inconceivable that some detail might pop up one day, and with it a whole new story, so, until then, I wait.

Which brings me to another very important aspect of mudlarking: patience. As archaeologist Ivor Noël Hume, the father of modern mudlarking, writes in his seminal 1956 book *Treasure in the Thames*: "The river-side antiquary must change his temperament to suit new conditions, needing the

18th–20th century clay pipes

patience of an angler who sets out with rod and line, but is content to catch a minnow."

In this case, Hume was referring to mudlarks adapting to the diminishing frequency of mind-blowing finds, which as recently as 1950 were often simply sitting pretty on the surface at every low tide. By 1955, easily discoverable artefacts in the "river's trinket box, opened for the first time soon after the Second World War" were diminishing due to "en masse foraging".

Mudlarking for pleasure is not a recent phenomenon. The Thames has long been scoured for objects of age and importance, both organic and man-made. The first half of the above Hume quote goes like this: "The prospect of mudlarking is not too bright, for too many people have tried their hand at it." But I think there's still a plethora of finds to salvage if you know where and how to look – and if you have the patience. ☺

Eight tips for novice mudlarkers

1. Anyone wishing to search the Thames foreshore must purchase a permit from the Port of London Authority (PLA).
2. If you'd like to try mudlarking before buying a permit, you can book a foreshore session with Steve Brooker, aka Mud God, at thamesandfield.com.
3. Study any relevant documents available on the PLA website. It's your responsibility to know where and how you are permitted to search the foreshore.
4. Respect your surroundings. Always know where your nearest exit is. If it's an upright ladder, make sure it's fully attached to the wall, and that you can climb it.
5. Kit yourself out properly. The foreshore can be a hazardous place – think slippery, sharp, trippy-over things.
6. Don't expect to get to grips with mudlarking in a day. It takes persistence to become accustomed to searching and finding – also known as "getting your eye in".
7. All mudlarks have a responsibility to record any items of treasure or significant historical value to the British Museum's Portable Antiquities Scheme.
8. Remember, although social media mudlarking forums can be fantastic, nothing beats books, historic publications and, most importantly, talking to people with experience. It might take time to make meaningful connections, but once you're in, you're in for life.

Early 20th century lead toys

Feature
Go with the Flow

Outdoor swimming pioneer **Kate Rew**
on sloshing, floating and drifting

JUST AS THERE was a time before triathlons, skateboarding, surfing, mountaineering or mountain biking, there was a time when mass-participation open-water swims were not commonplace. That time was pre-2006. In the grip of a love for adventurous swimming, and eager (messianic in fact) to get more people out of pools and into British rivers and lakes with me, I set up Breastrokes, a one-mile charity swim, and I chose the two best-known lakes I could think of (perhaps the only two lakes I could think of) in which to host it: the Serpentine in the middle of London, and Windermere in the Lake District.

The newly formed Outdoor Swimming Society (OSS) sold 300 tickets to each event. Finding 300 people with the same desire to swim – *in a lake* – drew gasps of surprise and column inches everywhere in Britain. In Windermere, swimmers docked at an island for hot chocolate halfway around, where people sloshed about in the shallows exclaiming how incredible it was, this outlandish, maverick thing they were doing. No one trained in a lake for the swims; they got fit in a pool and came for the novelty.

The Outdoor
Swimming Society

Kate swimming through the so-called
Death Valley on Burgh Island
off the Devon coast

A Dip into the Past

The first book on the theory and techniques of swimming was presented to the world in 1587 by Cambridge don Everard Digby in his *De Arte Natandi* ("The Art of Swimming"). Some of the advice in it is still valid: avoid murky ponds in which animals have been washed, and be careful about jumping in feet first. The book includes various woodcuts showing people swimming in a river that's banked by reeds and oak trees. The strokes may have changed, but the human urge to enjoy watercourses in the great outdoors looks much the same as it does today.

The earliest record of swimming, however, dates back much further, and is depicted on the walls of a cave in the mountainous Gilf Kebir plateau in Egypt. There, three figures are buoyed up by what appears to be the sluice and joy of a downstream Neolithic doggy paddle. The rock-art figures – whose creation is dated by the British Museum to about 6,000 to 9,000 years ago – carry with them all the happiness of a river float: arms up, bellies and spirits buoyant.

In 2006, the newly formed OSS, similarly uplifted by the swimming experience, set out a manifesto to help people escape chlorine captivity, leading with the pledge that we would "celebrate and enlarge the beauty of every day by going for a nice, long swim" (with a nod to the John Cheever story "The Swimmer"). Our focus ever since has been to persuade people to follow suit. An ever-growing band of individuals got involved: someone created a website, someone took photos, someone else bought a hot tub and everyone went swimming. Our lawyer, Nathan Willmott, wrote a Swim Responsibly Statement so we could come out in public and say, "Let's go swimming!" without fear of losing our homes. (This was a time when outdoor swimming was largely thought to be a dirty, dangerous and illegal activity, and there was fear of being sued.)

Lazy Old River

At its simplest, a river or stream is a body of water that flows only in one direction, from source to mouth. A river develops as it journeys, much like us. It begins small and clear-skinned, bright-eyed and magical: a bundle of energy moving fast over rocky riverbeds and tumbling down waterfalls.

Gradually it grows in size and presence – there can be some tricky teenage years, caught between weirs and a city centre, between being shallow and deep – but in time a river can grow big and warm and stately, and start to encompass you as a swimmer, putting its arms around you and carrying you along. Find an old river meandering through water meadows and you'll find a river that knows where it is going. There's no need to hurry.

Kate in a moment from the short film *Chasing the Sublime* (2018) directed by Amanda Bluglass

AA Milne's Christopher Robin thought that if he "watched the river slipping slowly away beneath him, then he would suddenly know everything that there was to be known". That's how it can feel to be in a mature river. Like all your messiness is taken away, leaving you meandering along with it, mind empty of all that doesn't matter and full of a wordless unarticulated sense of what does. Transcendent wisdom tends to evaporate like beads of water on skin when we exit, but if we're lucky we can still come home smelling of river water and sunshine, relaxed and content.

As you may be able to tell, I have a deep love of mature rivers – quasi-spiritual, neopagan, till-I-die love. I love the softness – of air and fresh water. The sense of going somewhere without having to dream it or will it myself (what a gift). The gentle pull downstream and all that goes with it: floating along, feeling buoyant, going with the flow. I like being immersed in the landscape – sunk down and made part of it. I'm a lover of the lonely landscape, and the fact that man-made mess – houses, roads, pylons, cars – often disappears behind a foreground of reeds, bushy banks and trees, leaving just the things that are wild in view, is a win for me. I like that my nose is pressed into the roots of nature – environmentalist Roger Deakin's "frog's-eye" view of the world – without attracting stares because I'm on my belly in mud. River swimming is about absorption on all levels: of us into nature and landscape, and nature into us.

Relax and Float Downstream
Who says you can't "go out for a swim" and then just lie back and float? Floating is the start of all swimming. We can all float; our lungs are like two balloons and if we relax and fill them up with air, they buoy us up. It's harder to float when muscles are tense. It's easier to float when we're relaxed,

49

confident and breathing deeply. The more body fat we have, the easier it is. Men often find it harder. It's easier to float in the sea, as salt water is denser than fresh.

Many teachers use floating as a building block to teaching people to swim, and as part of helping them overcome a learnt fear of the water. Floating is a fun and graceful pastime. Let's bring it back.

Stroke of Genius

Sidestroke is a wonderful style of swimming to have in your armoury. I find it a very soothing stroke when I'm in a wetsuit, all tired out and still not home: I like to rest my cheek on the surface of the water like a silk-cold pillow, stretch out and scissor-kick. It's a good stealth stroke; a variation (combat sidestroke) is used by Navy SEALS and the SAS for its low profile in the water and quiet non-splashiness. Outdoor swimmers can use it to approach wildlife quietly without causing alarm.

Sidestroke enables steady progress, and long distances can be covered with it. It's a good stroke to do on both sides – when one side gets tired, you can switch over while it recovers. It can be useful if you have injured one arm, or are struggling to put your face in very cold water, but want to get moving.

Sidestroke is used in lifesaving to tow people – variations of this include a cross-chest tow, where an arm is laid across the casualty with a hand just under an armpit, and an extended tow, where the hand is cupped under an unconscious casualty's chin and they are towed along that way.

Sea of Tranquillity

Rather than focusing on distance, speed or technique, many swimmers just like going out for an "aquatic stroll": a pleasant swim to see things, with focus both above and/or below the water. There's a whole subaquatic world down there to rival our terranean one. In 1972 Geoffrey Fraser Dutton published a

A moment of reflection in the river

Finisterre Microadventure 2020

book called *Swimming Free: On and Below the Surface of Lake, River and Sea*. In passionate and poetic detail, he shared the endless harmonies he saw, of light and plant and fish and water. Yes, we may see these things in tanks, books and rock pools. But "once immersed," he observed, "you are included." It's a very different experience. Dutton loved being released from the tyranny of gravity, savouring the joys of weightlessness "without infringing outer space". In water, we sense and sway with the wildlife we watch.

Dutton floated far out on the sun-smacked waves around the Highlands of Scotland, lay among the trout in the peaty shadows of a Highland river, drifted home over kelp beds on an evening tide – all the time focused on what lay beneath. "A stark glacial trench [is] as rewarding to the connoisseur of swimming as the most polychromatic tropical shelf," he observed after a swim in grey Loch Quoich.

It's not just big things; if you're curious, time spent studying freshwater invertebrates can be fascinating. Ecologist Peter Hancock says that if you listen quietly enough you can hear lesser water boatmen chirping.

Extracted from The Outdoor Swimmer's Handbook *by Kate Rew,
published by Ebury, £22*

Poetry
Three Wolf Fables

by Tara Bergin

Wolf and Cat

When the wolf runs from the forest into the village it is not for a visit.
He needs to save himself because his behavioural skin is trembling.
He no longer feels substantial. He looks for an opening but all the
gates are closed.

The wolf sees a cat sitting on the fence.

Vassenka! calls the wolf. Where can I hide from those vicious dogs?

What dogs? says the cat. I don't hear any dogs.

I do, says the wolf. They are tearing me apart.

Wolf and Fox

Sometimes the truth is more bearable when it is only half-open.
(That's how the story of cruelty began).

Wolf and Eyes

One night while the wolf was sleeping the sheep gathered together to carry out a plan. They crept into the lair, stole the wolf's eyes, and stuck them onto his back legs. Then they crept away without the wolf even moving a muscle.

In the morning the wolf killed the sheep as usual.

But for once he saw the damage he'd done in hindsight.

Tara Bergin is from Dublin and has published two collections of poetry with Carcanet Press. The "Three Wolf Fables" that appear here come from her third book, which is due to be published in Autumn 2022

STYLE

Slow Fashion
A Bigger Splash

Immerse yourself in style this summer with our selection of sustainable swim, surf and beach wear, chosen by **Alice Smith**

Long Sleeve Reversible Winter Suit
by Davy J
For those brave enough to go
wild swimming.
Material: Neoprene
Women's sizes: 6–20
£160
davyj.com

Bikini and zip-up swimsuit
by Stay Wild
Women's sizes: 6–24
£50–£170
staywildswim.com

Swimsuits
by Usual Objections
For loud and proud swimmers.
And for dog lovers, a customised dog portrait
design option.
Women's sizes: XXS–XXXXXL
£85–£125
usualobjections.com

Swimming shorts
by Riz
Statement shorts include this Endangered Bee design,
and a William Morris-style pattern with a sea theme.
Men's sizes 30–38 / S–XXL
£90–£100
rizboardshorts.com

Swimsuits
by Tucca
Two designs for the price of one with Tucca's Multiway
reversible range.
Women's sizes: XS–XL
£44–£115
tuccaswim.co.uk

Swimsuits by Batoko
Recycled plastic never looked so good
as when made into these fun and
cheery swimsuits.
Women's sizes: XS–XXXL
£60
batoko.com

Idle Home
A Rye Tale

*Georgina Williams visits a former St John Ambulance station in Rye
that's been restored to architectural life as a stylish holiday home
Photos by* **Voytek Ketz**

THROUGHOUT HISTORY THE East Sussex coast has been subject to dramatic change. The relentless energy of the English Channel, coupled with ferocious storms in the Middle Ages, radically altered its landscape, transforming the tidal creeks and salt marshes and redrawing the coastline to submerge some settlements, while leaving others high and dry.

One of the settlements that remained unscathed was Rye. Situated on top of a sandstone outcrop, it was afforded natural protection from the sea, while the surrounding marshland provided a rich bounty for its inhabitants. The coast had once been linked to France by a land bridge and although physically parted for thousands of years, a powerful

House style: the former station retains much of its original character

connection remained.

While this was sometimes useful in the case of trade, it was more often turbulent and violent, with a constant threat of invasion. From 1017, for more than 200 years, Rye was ruled by the Abbey of Fécamp in Normandy and, on its return to English rule in 1247, its future remained precarious and defences were stepped up. A wall and four gates were built to form a citadel and when a particularly violent storm ravaged the coast in 1287, it altered the course of the River Rother, creating a new outlet at Rye and a natural harbour ideal for mooring a protective fleet.

The town began to flourish, providing ships and men for the King, and in 1336 this "cradle of the navy" was made a Cinque Port, bringing further prosperity and freedom to its inhabitants.

By the beginning of the 16th century, however, the sea had receded almost two miles from Rye and the marsh that emerged was drained to create pasture for grazing sheep. This avenue of income only profited the wealthy landowners; for the average inhabitants of Rye, earning a living was tough. Smuggling was enticing and lucrative for many and the narrow streets and dark headlands enabled this illegal trade to flourish here well into the 18th century.

To walk the streets today is to sense a little of this history.

With their paths dictated by the historic footprint of fortifications, the concentric streets loop the summit of this mediaeval town. Lined with ancient buildings and bisected by alleyways, every now and then they open up to reveal incredible views out across the marshes or to the hills.

On one of these cobbled thoroughfares, close to Landgate (the only gate that remains), lies a courtyard set back from the street. Behind the wall sit two strangely compatible dwellings; to one side an elegant Georgian house, and to the other a restrained, almost covert, property – St John.

Marta Nowicka, an award-winning interior architect, came across St John a decade ago when she was living just down the road in Camber Sands. It had originally been built in the 1950s as a large garage and workshop for the St John Ambulance Brigade. In the 1970s it had been extended to accommodate their offices and a kitchen, but by the turn of the century the St John Ambulance had moved on and the building had fallen into disrepair.

Marta is an expert at breathing life into disused commercial buildings and she could immediately sense its potential. To enter St John today is to experience her expertise and scrupulous consideration of place, material and history.

After a protracted debate, Marta

secured planning to remove the 1970s extension and replace it with a double height space to link the first and second floors with a new staircase. This freed up room in the original building as well as creating two additional bedrooms and bathrooms. The result is a great success; the external walls are hung with handmade clay peg tiles and the roof pitch is marginally lower so that it sits quietly next to the primary structure, as well as the surrounding buildings. The garage doors, which span the front of the building, were removed and artfully reproduced to meet building requirements. The soft red brick walls were cleaned and the clay tiles were removed from the twin gables but reinstated complete with moss in situ. From the outside, this building has been so sensitively converted that there is no dramatic, discernible change.

Stepping into the entrance hall in the new extension, you are immediately struck by the light and by the harmonious relationship between the interior and exterior – captured by generous steel-framed windows, which give views out to

New walls have been covered with oak boards, matching the floor

[above] The huge windows allow in plenty of light

[right] View from the staircase

the old brick perimeter wall. The bottom stairs are cast concrete with a rather beautiful pocked surface (a happy accident which occurred during setting) while the remaining flight has open steel treads and a simple rope balustrade to allow as much light as possible to filter through. It's a calm but practical space, with a deep storage chest and Shaker-esque peg rail fitted to one side, as well as a useful downstairs shower-room and bedroom tucked cleverly to the rear of the stairs.

The real showstopper though is

63

Brick walls have been left exposed to reveal the building's history

the original space. Marta removed the dividing wall between the old muster station and garage to create a single open-plan living space. There is now a sleek kitchen area to one side and a relaxing sitting area on the other – perfect for unwinding or entertaining. The two zones are visually linked by a central double-sided wood burner; a nod to the mediaeval hall houses of the area where the hearth was positioned at the centre of the home.

The rear wall is clad in riven oak, echoing the kitchen cabinets and cleverly emphasising the feeling of space with a seamless line of colour and texture.

Marta saved the original garage doors and sanded them back to mellow pine. They now lean against the wall in the dining area where they add warmth and interest. The dining table is a fine lesson in salvage; spying a vast timber washed up on Camber Sands, Marta persuaded a contractor moving shingle to help her bring it back to her cottage, where she planned its future. She designed a table of loose planks that can easily be removed and altered to make one long table for feasting, or remain a more compact square for everyday use. There was enough left over to make two sturdy bedside tables for the downstairs bedroom and these are currently topped with a pair of

The salvaged timber dining table and sleek kitchen area, with garage doors behind
[below] The lounging space

lamps ingeniously made from the champagne bottles used to celebrate the end of the build.

Upstairs, the family bathroom is tucked under the eaves and again Marta's attention to detail and thoughtfulness is evident. The design of the porcelain floor tiles echoes the emblem of the St John Ambulance, while the sink stand and storage chest are made from reclaimed medical cabinets, also alluding to this past narrative.

On the landing of the original upper floor the brick walls have been restored and left exposed to proudly reveal their scars and patina. New walls are clad in oak,

The atmosphere is one of calmness and continuity

echoing the ground floor finish and emphasising an atmosphere of continuity and calm. In Marta's hands this attic space is no longer cramped; under-eaves storage has been removed, increasing the feeling of space, while inventive new glazing – one large pane slipped cleverly into the valley between the two gables – gives fine views out across the town and to the hills beyond.

This is an Idle Home with deep respect for and a constant connection to its history and surroundings. One that quietly observes its past while embracing the future as a contemporary, practical family home. It's an important building much loved by the community – many of whom retain a sense of ownership having trained here in their youth. In transforming St John, Marta has honoured this sensibility and created an incredibly relaxing space to stay and to gather – a building with real integrity which definitely provides a good dose of first aid for the soul. ☻

Buy George

Stay at St John
Marta established her concept-led studio in 2003 to find design solutions for commercial and residential spaces. Visit her website DOM Stay & Live to view some of the other projects she has designed, including The Gouse, a three-bedroom house built on the site of a dilapidated garage at the end of a garden in Dalston, East London. Here she has also curated a unique collection of architecturally interesting, award-winning homes, which are available to rent. All of them meet her rigorous criteria and can be booked direct on the website, enabling you to stay at jaw-dropping lake-side pods in Scandinavia, fabulous villas in Italy and Spain, as well as a number of her own projects in the UK, including St John. **domstayandlive.com**

On Altering Architecture by Fred Scott (£35 online)
Scott was a tutor at Kingston School of Art and a great inspiration to Marta when she studied Interior Architecture there. His landmark text *On Altering Architecture* examines the craft of altering existing buildings, reconsidering ideas and methods and exploring the development of architectural interiors. It's available from the RIBA bookshop. **ribabooks.com**

Handmade Clay Tiles
The handmade clay peg tiles used on the extension at St John were made in the traditional manner just down the coast by Tudor Roof Tiles in Lydd. They have a catalogue of styles they make to order. I particularly like the innovative Bat Access Set. **tudorrooftiles.co.uk**

Textiles
Merchant & Mills is situated just around the corner from St John in Tower Street. It was established in 2010 by Carolyn Denham and Roderick Field with the aim of bringing style and purpose to the world of sewing. They sell beautiful, unique fabrics from around the world as well as a compelling range of haberdashery oddments, patterns and tools. Their heavyweight fabrics and vintage textiles are perfect for upholstery. **merchantandmills.com**

Puckhaber Decorative Antiques
I have long admired the Puckhaber stand at the Decorative Antique Fair in Battersea so it was thrilling to visit their country HQ. This mother-and-son partnership specialises in original painted furniture and continental decorative antiques. They have a shop on Lillie Road in west London and a second outpost at No 1 High Street in Rye. **puckhaberdecorativeantiques.com**

Lamb House
Visit Lamb House in Rye. Built in 1722, it was once home to the American novelist Henry James and was where he wrote his most acclaimed novels. EF Benson, a friend of James and one-time Mayor of Rye, also lived at the house from 1919 until his death in 1940. He was a prolific writer of fiction and set his Mapp and Lucia novels in a seaside town based on Rye, with Lamb House as "Mallards", the home of Miss Mapp. **nationaltrust.org.uk**

Rye Castle Museum
Situated in the Ypres Tower, once part of the important fortifications built to protect the town, Rye Castle Museum has an interesting collection and stunning views over Romney Marsh. Of particular note however is the reconstruction of a 15th-century pleasure garden stocked with important culinary and medicinal herbs. **ryemuseum.co.uk**

The Good Stuff

Our regular register of booming businesses by
Annabel Sampson *and* Charlotte Brook

Born to Rewild

Set up by pioneers of the rewilding movement, Isabella Tree and Charles Burrell, Knepp Wild Range Meat is something a bit special. The Knepp estate in West Sussex is a former arable and dairy farm that has been rewilded and is now home to Longhorn cattle, Tamworth pigs, and red and fallow deer. All of the animals are free to roam the 3,500-acre site, feeding the way nature intended them to – not on so-called "performance feeds" and grains. The result is meat that is produced in a sustainable, low-cost and very low-carbon way. It's also delicious. Well worth supporting, we say.

kneppwildrangemeat.co.uk

Image © Charles Burrell of the Knepp estate

King of the Swingers

Imagine having your favourite sofa in your garden all summer long. That's the premise behind Old Rockers – luxury garden swing seats created by outdoor furniture makers ODD. Cushioned, tasselled and colourful as a Maharaja's throne, frankly there's nowhere the Good Stuff would rather sit than on one of these decadent, handmade swinging sofas. What's more, they're bespoke – you choose the colour and fabric – and yes, the fabrics are waterproof – as well as details such as whether to have a scalloped or straight roof, with fringing or piping, or topped with regal ball finials… Browse their website and then call them to discuss how you'd like yours made. *oddlimited.com*

Slow Tech
Instant Camera!

Taking instant photos can be a lot of fun, producing timeless miniature works of art. But which is better – Polaroid or Instax?
Lee Osborne puts you in the picture

THE REVIVED INTEREST in analogue technology has seen instant photography becoming really popular again after a few lean years. In the past, Polaroid was the only game in town if you wanted to see your photos straight away, and even in the instant-feedback era of digital photography, there's something special about a unique, one-off picture developing before your eyes.

Instant photos are little works of art that can't easily be reproduced, and it's no surprise that famous creators like Andy Warhol and Ansel Adams were big fans. I've shot plenty of instant photos myself lately, and despite a few frustrations here and there, I've had a lot of fun with Polaroid and Instax cameras.

Polaroid is, of course, synonymous with instant photography in the same way that Hoover is with vacuum cleaners. It remains one of the two analogue instant photography systems available today, although the company had a chequered history, and Polaroid cameras and film almost disappeared entirely in the early 2000s. A heroic attempt to revive Polaroid photography was successful, and the brand has re-established itself in a big way in the last few years.

Polaroid cameras were pioneered by Edwin Land, a scientist with a dogged determination to produce the perfect instant camera. It's rumoured he started work on inventing them after he took a photo of his daughter, and she asked why she couldn't see the picture right away. The first Polaroid Land Camera was unveiled in 1948. Back then, using these cameras was a fiddly business involving peel-apart layers that had to be separated after careful timing, and the user risked being exposed to a nasty caustic paste. Despite these problems, millions were sold, with demand taking the company by surprise.

It took Land until 1972 to achieve the breakthrough he wanted – a camera that automatically ejected a picture that would develop perfectly without any further intervention. This was the SX-70 system, and the birth of Polaroid photos as most of us will remember – a square image with white borders, the border much thicker along the bottom. The improved 600 film followed, and all was well until the 1990s, when sales dropped sharply and the company ran into serious financial trouble. In the early 2000s, the company declared bankruptcy twice and was eventually broken up. Production of film ceased in 2008, and after that the Polaroid brand merely appeared on consumer electronics products made by other companies.

All was not lost, however. The last surviving Polaroid film factory, in the Netherlands, was scheduled for demolition, along with its unique machinery, but was saved at the last

minute by The Impossible Project, a group dedicated to reviving Polaroid photography. The members used the factory to start producing new films in 2010. They faced considerable challenges, and had to reformulate the films from scratch. Early Impossible Project films were very unstable, but they've improved a lot since then.

The Impossible Project was able to licence the Polaroid brand and sell films under the Polaroid Originals name from 2017, launching a new camera at the same time. They're now sold as Polaroid films once more. The reformulation has, however, made them rather different from the older products. There are now only eight pictures to a pack rather than ten (the new ones are slightly thicker than the old), and there's a couple of things you need to watch when shooting them. First, the pictures don't develop well in low temperatures, so you'll need to put them in a warm pocket if you shoot in cold weather. Second, they can be damaged if exposed to light in the first few minutes after they pop out of the camera. This can be dealt with quite easily, though – see my hints and tips section. Black and white film is less prone to these issues.

Polaroid photos have a particularly timeless look to them, with a warm, soft tone to the colours, and a lo-fi appearance that looks stunning when you pick the right subject. It can be tricky getting good results, and mistakes are costly, but once you know how to get the best out of the film, it can be very rewarding to use.

The film is available in SX-70 and 600 formats for older cameras – these film packs have built-in batteries to power the camera. Newer cameras released since Polaroid's revival have their own batteries, and can use i-Type film. This is slightly cheaper as it doesn't need the built-in battery, but cannot be used in vintage cameras.

Plenty of special editions of Polaroid film are made, with different borders, and there's also Duochrome, a tinted monochrome film available in blue and yellow versions. I love the bold look this film creates.

The most recent addition to the Polaroid line-up is Polaroid Go, a camera that produces much smaller pictures, and which is claimed to be the smallest instant camera available. It's clearly aimed at competing with Instax Mini, a system very popular with young people.

For a brief period in the seventies and eighties, Kodak sold their own instant cameras and film, but Polaroid immediately sued them for copyright infringement. Kodak lost the extremely bitter, expensive and long-running court case that resulted, and was forced to stop

making the system.

Some years later, however, Fuji somehow got away with launching an instant photography system of their own, Instax, which Polaroid didn't seem too bothered about. It launched in Japan in 1998, and became available worldwide shortly afterwards.

Three different sizes of camera and film are available. The smallest is Instax Mini – credit card sized, portrait-format images produced by a wide range of compact and colourful cameras, aggressively marketed at teenagers. These have become hugely popular. Slightly bigger is Instax Square. These look very similar to Polaroid photos (similar enough for the company to grumble about copyright again when they were launched), but are somewhat smaller.

The biggest format is Instax Wide. The photos are the same size as classic Polaroids, but rotated 90 degrees for a landscape-format picture. The cameras are big and unwieldy, but I think this is my favourite instant photography format.

As well as Fuji's own camera models, several other companies make instant cameras using Instax film, so the choice is huge.

Instax cameras are very different from Polaroids. Firstly, the photos emerge from the top rather than the front. The developed results are somewhat different too, with more contrast and brighter colours. You also don't need to worry about light exposure or cold when the pictures emerge, so they could be a better choice if you regularly shoot in difficult conditions.

To give you an idea of how differently Instax and Polaroid can render the same scene, here are two shots of Salisbury Crags in Edinburgh. The square picture was shot with a Polaroid Button camera from the early 1980s, on SX-70 film, and the other was taken with an Instax Wide 100.

You'll see that the Polaroid has less contrast, and that the sky and parts of the landscape have very different tints to them. I think it's fair to say the Instax has produced a technically much better picture, but the Polaroid has perhaps rendered the scene a bit more dreamily.

Vintage Polaroid cameras exist in vast quantities and I've yet to find one that doesn't work. Check to make sure it uses SX-70 or 600 film, as some film formats have been discontinued. If you'd rather buy a new one, several i-Type models are available from Polaroid, which have the advantage of using the lower-priced film packs.

Unfortunately, Polaroid photos are very expensive to shoot, costing over two pounds each at normal retail price. Instax is somewhat cheaper, with Mini

Snap decisions: the InstaxWide photo is more accurate...

... but the Polaoroid has perhaps more charm is more accurate...

photos typically costing about 70p each, going up to just over a pound for the bigger Wide format. If you shoot Polaroid regularly though, you can buy film direct from the company's website. It offers a generous loyalty scheme, so it's possible to rack up discounts pretty quickly, especially if you buy a camera from there too.

Hints and Tips for Successful Instant Photography

Whichever format you're using, instant pictures need lots of light to look good. Always shoot in the brightest light you can, and use flash if possible. Bright sunny days are the best.

The majority of instant cameras are completely automatic, but most Polaroids and some Instax cameras have lighten/darken controls. If your first attempt doesn't look right, experiment with these to see if you prefer the results.

Evenly lit scenes produce much better results than ones with contrasting light and dark areas. Shoot colourful scenes for eye-popping pictures.

If shooting with a vintage Polaroid, buy a replacement film tongue (available from the Polaroid website) to protect your pictures while they're developing. They come with fitting instructions.

Use fresh film. Expired instant film deteriorates very quickly, and most of the time it won't work at all.

There's a lot of old Polaroid film on eBay, but most of it is a waste of money.

Keep film in the fridge before loading it into your camera, but don't freeze it or you'll ruin the developing chemicals.

Books and Other Resources

Polaroid photos have become such cultural icons that there are lots of books to inspire and inform the instant photo snapper. *The Polaroid Book*, edited by Steve Crist, contains a fantastic array of Polaroid photos specially curated and collected by the company – cameras and films were given away to photographers and artists to encourage serious creative use. Sadly the collection was broken up and sold off when the company hit hard times, but this book shows off some of the best examples from it. Also well worth a look are *Instant: The Story of Polaroid* by Christopher Bonanos, and *Polaroid: The Magic Material* by Florian Kaps, which tells the story of Polaroid's rescue and relaunch.

Websites can be found for the two systems at polaroid.com and instax.com. There's also a huge market in secondhand Polaroid cameras, which can frequently be found on eBay and in charity shops. ◉

Twentieth
Century
Society

Love architecture?

The C20 Society leads the way in campaigning to protect significant architecture, design and public art from 1914 onwards. With members' support, important buildings such as Preston Bus Station (above) and Battersea Power Station now have listing protection, and an economically viable future, but other important works remain at risk. Please consider donating to C20 Society or joining us. For more information about C20 architecture, full membership benefits, including our events programme and members magazine (right), please visit:
c20society.org.uk

ARTS & BOOKS

Art Flâneur
Ridiculously Good

Tim Richardson enters Heath Robinson's world of comically complicated constructions. Plus an essential Raphael exhibition at the National and the much-maligned genius Walter Sickert at Tate Britain

HAVE YOU BEEN to Pinner? It's a marvellous place. A dream of olde England, with half-timbered buildings (some "real", some 1930s), tree-lined lanes and a generally sunny disposition. And, handily for me, it's "in London" – sort of. On the Metropolitan Line, anyway, in that curious, semi-fake suburban hinterland immortalised by John Betjeman as Metroland.

I was flâneuring around there because of William Heath Robinson (1872-1944), the artist and cartoonist, who lived in Pinner for a decade or so. His modest house on twisty Moss Lane has a blue plaque commemorating this fact, and, somewhat extraordinarily, there's a whole museum devoted to his work in the middle of the pleasant Pinner Memorial Park. The Heath Robinson Museum opened in 2016, funded by the Lottery. Designed by ZMMA architects, it is appropriately over-complex, with a copper-clad roof that appears to be falling in on itself, galleries described as "deformed rectangles" and witty internal details such as wormlike ventilation ducts and light fittings made of copper piping.

This summer (until 4 September) the museum is celebrating the 150th anniversary of Heath Robinson's birth with an exhibition focused on his humorous illustrations. These include the "contraption" cartoons which led to his surname becoming an adjective in fairly common usage – among the middle classes at any rate. In case you didn't know, it refers to any bodged-up or over-complicated homemade system for performing some mundane function. We all have a bit of Heath Robinson in our homes – I have a taped-together contraption in my attic which I created to disperse cigar fumes.

Heath Robinson also worked as a "serious" artist and illustrator, and the general curatorial focus at the museum has been to highlight the illustrations he provided to Shakespeare, Rabelais and children's books such as *The Water-Babies*. These can be very fine indeed, but it's almost as if his more humorous watercolours and drawings – which formed the bulk of his output from the 1920s, when the market for book illustrations started to dry up – are perceived as being of "second-order". I couldn't disagree more, partly because the cartoons are finished to the same level of detail as his "serious"

output, but mainly because the ability to create, repeatedly, illustrations that make you laugh out loud is vanishingly rare. As every performer and writer knows – and also some artists – comedy is the hardest thing to do of all, which is why it's so respected and cherished by people "in the business".

And Heath Robinson was very much "in the business". He learnt about the reality of the art world from his father, who had to produce a full-page illustration for the *Penny Post* without fail once a week for decades. Both of Heath Robinson's brothers were also professional (as in "jobbing") artists. There was no distinction, for them, between "serious" and "not-serious" work. It was just work.

The exhibition shows how Heath Robinson's humorous style was forged in World War I, when he started to produce cartoons that pricked the perceived pomposity of the Teutonic "Hun". He may depict Zeppelins in freefall, but the cartoons are never cruel. Heath Robinson always avoided politics as a topic. The world he creates is, like PG Wodehouse's, entirely without malice.

After the war Heath Robinson transferred his attentions to that great British bugbear, needless bureaucracy, where too many people spend too much time creating "solutions" that don't work. A typical contraption cartoon

He was also alive to trends in the art world; one rarely seen cartoon in the exhibition is a take on the Futurist manifesto. Indeed, much of Heath Robinson's later output can be perceived as a satire on modernity, especially in the guise of fantasy "labour-saving devices" and modern ways of living – one of his books was entitled *How to Live in a Flat* (1936).

World War II presented another opportunity for gently propagandic cartoons which seek to deflate our deepest fears of the enemy through ridicule, or by means of plucky ingenuity on the Home Front such as "the melted butter tank stopper",

Heath Robinson *German breaches of the Hague Convention – Huns using siphons of laughing gas to overcome our troops before an attack in close formation* (1915)

depicts an experimental laboratory or factory ground, peopled with pudgy, bespectacled boffins in baggy tweed suits who are all busy testing their gadgets in deadly earnest. Pipes, pulleys, flywheels and counterweights add needless complexity to relatively simple operations. Many of these devices require unfeasibly large numbers of people to operate, such as in *Testing Artificial Teeth in a Modern Tooth Works* (1929), where individual teeth are being subjected to minute scrutiny.

Heath Robinson *Testing artificial teeth in a modern tooth works* (1929)

Images © The Heath Robinson Museum

HOW TO TAKE ADVANTAGE OF THE SAVOY ORPHEAN DANCE MUSIC BROADCAST
BY THE B.B.C. · WITHOUT DISTURBING YOUR NEIGHBOUR
IN THE FLAT BELOW.

Heath Robinson's design for a silent disco (1928)

intended to stymie an invasion of Britain. But unlike in the first war, he didn't depict the enemy in person – he instinctively knew that the SS, for example, was not suitable subject matter for humour.

Heath Robinson's work also played on that very British fondness for "the boffin". As a result, we do have a kind of amused admiration for the contraptions. Was there not something rather Heath-Robinson about useful wartime improvisations such as the bouncing bomb, faked-up airfields or the Hobart's Funnies (specialised tanks)? The real wartime boffins loved these cartoons, too: when the Bletchley Park codebreakers came up with a complex new machine which turned out to be the precursor of the celebrated Colossus, they named it Heath Robinson.

In a strange twist, for me anyway, it turns out that the Heath Robinson family home where he grew up, a terrace house near Finsbury Park, is about 400 metres from where I live, right next door to my local pub. I will raise a toast to his

memory from now on, when in there, perhaps drinking it through an unnecessarily convoluted and complex homemade straw which transports the beer up my trouser leg, into the frame of my glasses, down through a false moustache and thence into my mouth.

Heath Robinson *Spring cleaning in Aberdeen* (1929)

There are a couple of other exhibitions on at the moment that can be highly recommended. *Raphael* at the National Gallery (until 31 July) is a proper old-school "blockbuster" which demands to be seen. It's packed with major works from every phase of the artist's development, from the beautifully serene Madonnas of his Florence period, to the mature output in Rome, in which his female figures seem less ethereally virginal and more like the real women we know the artist loved.

There's a dream room of Madonnas – five in one gulp – and also the magnificent St Cecilia altarpiece from Bologna. I think people thought I'd fallen to my knees in front of this picture, which

Raphael
The Alba Madonna (about 1509–11)

shows the saint surrounded by discarded musical instruments and a wonderfully expressive supporting cast of saints in robes of azure, gold, grey and pink. I was only trying to get a better idea of the correct perspective, as the painting was designed for a high altar, not to be shown at conventional gallery height, as here. It's much better viewed from a prostrate position, if you don't mind making an exhibition of yourself.

The curators haven't followed the recent trend of fleshing out shows by including works by those who influenced the artist, or were themselves influenced. This is all about Raphael. There are numerous sketches on the walls, revealing not only Raphael's dynamism as an artist (which isn't always apparent in the finished full-sized works) but also provide glimpses of the kinds of

Raphael *The Garvagh Madonna*

81

paintings he could have produced if given the opportunity; for example, the battle scene known as the *Siege of Perugia* is bursting with energy and movement. The sheer intensity of these working drawings shows that it wasn't all effortless for Raphael, as has been supposed.

More of an acquired taste, perhaps, is the surprisingly expansive Walter Sickert exhibition at Tate Britain (until 18 September). Even now Sickert's output is being described as "murky" or "dingy" in reviews, while there is excessive and prurient emphasis on an unfounded accusation by an American crime novelist that he was Jack the Ripper. Don't let this put you off unduly.

Walter Sickert *Gallery of the Old Bedford* (1894–5)

Sickert was a great artist who trained with Whistler and Degas and whose, admittedly variable, output can on occasion vie with that of the most celebrated of the French Impressionists. Sickert was able to translate the liveliness and immediacy of his sketches into finished works in oil paint – which not even the best artists always manage to do. His thickly applied paint tends to look drab in reproductions, but in real life its subtleties and, importantly, texture can be appreciated, in works such as *L'Eldorado* (*c*.1906), which depicts a Parisian theatre interior with its gilded balconies.

Sickert's theatricality is brought out consistently in the exhibition – in his self-portraiture, in which he appears in different guises, and also in his use of the music hall as a subject. Sickert lived on Mornington Crescent in London and regularly painted both audience and performers at the Old Bedford theatre, which was around the corner on Camden High Street. There are numerous fine examples of his music-hall pictures in the exhibition, including the large and spectacular *The New Bedford* (1907) from Leeds Art Gallery.

Perhaps it was this sense of theatricality which led to what now appears to have been a spectacularly ill-advised decision by Sickert to name or rename some of his paintings of women in bedrooms to

Image © Walker Art Gallery

Walter Sickert *Self portrait* (c.1896)

paintings are possessed of a voyeuristic quality which can lead to a certain queasiness. But no more than in the work of other painters of the period, such as Bonnard or Vuillard. In several of Sickert's paintings, the women are simply lying there, sometimes smiling and apparently relaxed. The men depicted are not necessarily evil or murderous, though they are sometimes clothed when the women are not. They may be clients of the working women, and as such could be seen as "predators", but it doesn't follow that they're murderers. Quite why Sickert decide to reframe his paintings in this genre with

reference the Camden Town Murder of 1907, which clearly affected him deeply. The artist's motive for doing this remains unclear – it could have been simple titillation, of the public as well as himself, or even a self-destructive impulse – but the result is that Sickert has since been unreasonably suspected of being some kind of murderer. It has undermined his entire reputation.

The basis for this accusation is that the women in his bedroom scenes – who are often nudes or in a state of undress – are murder victims, or are about to be murdered. It's true that the

Walter Sickert *La Hollandaise* (c.1906)

Hew Locke: *The Procession*

reference to a specific murder is a mystery, as is the habit of contemporary critics to make moralising judgments about the artist on the basis of zero evidence.

While you're in the Tate – or if you don't want to spend any money on a ticket – don't miss the astounding installation *The Procession* by Hew Locke (until 22 January), which extends the entire length of the Duveen Galleries. Consisting of hundreds of costumed mannequin figures, it's a true tour-de-force of installation art, possessed of an almost unbelievable level of detail and vigour. 👁

ART PREVIEW
Flâneur recommends

Radical Landscapes
Until 4 September
A subversive and psychedelic take on a traditionally conservative topic.
Tate Liverpool,
Albert Dock, Liverpool L3 4BB

Reframed: The Woman in the Window
Until 4 September
Intriguing thematic show, from Rembrandt to Cindy Sherman.
Dulwich Picture Gallery,
Gallery Road, London SE21 7AD

Dominique Gonzalez-Foerster: Alienarium 5
"A speculative environment that invites us to imagine possible encounters with extraterrestrials."
Until 4 September
Serpentine South Gallery,
Kensington Gardens, London W2 3XA

Cornelia Parker
Until 16 October
Total retro featuring films and embroidery as well as installation work.
Tate Britain,
Millbank, London SW1P 4RG

Uncombed, Unforeseen, Unconstrained
Until 27 November
Ambitious group show on the theme of entropy and environmental dismay.
Parasol Unit,
14 Wharf Road, London N1 7RW

Japan: Courts and Culture
Until 12 March
Still plenty of time to see this one.
The Queen's Gallery,
Buckingham Palace, London SW1A 1AA

Mysterious Albion

Cathi Unsworth hails a beautifully curated collection of dark and dreamlike images that show a history of England as seen through Dr Dee's scrying glass

England on Fire: A Visual Journey Through Albion's Psychic Landscape
Stephen Ellcock, Mat Osman
(Watkins, £25)

When I was three years old, my granddad took me to Ringstead Downs, a chalk gorge hidden deep in the Norfolk countryside. Vertiginous, tree-lined hills enclose a verdant pathway, burnished with the gold of buttercups, yellow rattle and hawkbit. In my memory there were deer there, the first I'd ever seen. Fifty years on, the magic of this secret place remains tangible. There is a point, on top of one hill, where I always expect to see a sentinel in the form of a man wearing stag's horns, just like the one depicted by Dan Hillier on the

cover of Stephen Ellcock's remarkable *England on Fire*.

Master curator Ellcock embeds this sense of continuity in the choice of images selected for this volume, presenting an artists'-eye view of our land and a poet's comprehension of its archeological layers. Thus, the stunning craftsmanship of an Anglo Saxon brooch sits alongside punk artefacts by Jamie Reid and Derek Jarman; work by contemporary artists with whom you may not yet be familiar stands shoulder-to-shoulder with the Old Gods also present: Blake and Beardsley, Hogarth and Stanley Spencer.

Our haunted landscape is viewed in photos, paintings and film stills: Paul Nash's 1944 *Landscape of the Vernal Equinox III* next to stills from Derek Jarman's 1973 *A Journey to Avebury*; Spencer Gore's 1912 *The Icknield Way*, Eric Ravilious's 1939 *The Vale of White Horse* and Bill Brandt's silver gelatin print of *The Pilgrims' Way* (1950). Folkloric traditions are seen in photographs of Abbots Bromley horn dancers from

Paul Nash *Landscape of the Vernal Equinox III* (1944)

1900; Longparish mummers some 20 years later; and a spooktacular lithograph of Lewes Bonfire Boys from 1853 by Thomas Henwood. Cathy Ward's awesomely intricate ink-on-gold *Corn Maiden* (2015) summons the Goddess of the Fields; John Douglas Piper's wonderful *Black Shuck* series makes effigies of the Demon Dog from objects found on East Anglian farms in 2019.

Taking a fortean approach to his survey, Ellcock includes work from automatic painters Madge Gill (*Untitled*, 1945), who is said to have connected with her spirit guide after the death of her daughter in 1920; and Georgiana Houghton (*The Portrait of the Lord Jesus Christ*, 1862), whose work impacted on the Surrealists. Then he contrasts them

with the "ghost photography" of WS Hobson, whose 1887 image pokes fun at a Victorian obsession. The fae folk at the bottom of the garden are captured by Arthur Rackham, Richard Dadd, Richard Doyle and the infamous duo Elsie Wright and Frances Griffiths, who fooled Sir Arthur Conan Doyle with their cut-out Cottingley Fairies of 1917. There's also arguably the first image of a crop circle – *The Mowing-Devil: or, Strange News out of Hartford-Shire*, a woodcut pamphlet of 1678, which illustrates a mysterious precursor to the phenomena, in this case being made by Satan himself.

How different the past can appear: a wicker man much like the one in which Christopher Lee roasted

Derek Jarman, stills from A Journey to Avebury (1973)

Edward Woodward looms out of John Warner Barber's 1860 imagining of *Romans Destroying the Druids* – however, the Romans resemble Arthurian knights and the druids Cardinal Wolsey. Whereas the big daddy of spirit painting, Austin Osman Spare, presents his pagan holy men as shaven-headed, lurching zombies in his 1955 *Druidesque*. Elsewhere in time, and no less disorientating, George Baxter captures Benjamin Waterhouse Hawkins' Crystal Palace dinosaurs in 1864 like a scene from a south London *Jurassic Park*.

Sometimes these images hit us with the shock of the old: Samuel Palmer's 1825 *Early Morning* resembles an illustration from a 1970s children's book; while

William O'Keefe's 1796 caricature of Pitt the Younger, with the sun looking on with the face of a bored Eric Cantona, is not dissimilar in intent from the work of Jamie Reid (*When the Earth Had Many Moons*, *Curse English Heritage*, both 1990). Ellcock delights in such timeshifts.

I found pure delight in the unexpected here – Yorkshire's Lord of Darkness, John Atkinson Grimshaw suddenly bursting into golden light in 1884's *Evening Glow*. Two of my favourite "new" artists are musicians I first met when they made equally brilliant records in the early 1990s. Gallon Drunk's James F Johnston captures sunset in a forest grove on *Parade* (2019) and a robed figure in *Garden* (2021) who could be a ghostly nun or grey lady.

Cathy Ward Corn Maiden (2015)

While Johnston's paintings have the luminosity of stained glass, artist and musician Pinkie Maclure actually works in this much-neglected medium. Her *Green Man Searches for Wilderness* (2020) shows the titular deity using binoculars to scry for traces of his vanishing realm. Another musician of this vintage, Suede's Mat Osman, provides the linking text.

Which all took me back to my stag-horned Herne the Hunter on Ringstead Downs – which you could dismiss as fanciful imagination. Except, this is the same landscape that gave up the Snettisham Hoard to a ploughman in 1948; close to where the sands shifted to reveal the Bronze Age Seahenge in 1998. I like to think of him as a memory from the ancestors, who venerated the stag and wore his horns in their rituals – like this wonderful book, a neural pathway back through England's dreaming. 🐌

Pinkie Maclure *Green Man Searches for Wilderness* (2020)

Books

Beyond Belief

*Rob Greer and Julia Lasica round up a selection of books
from the interzones between life and death,
countries and countryside*

Gargoyles **Harriet Mercer**
(Dead Ink, £9.99)

In the middle of the night in March 2008, jewellery shop owner Harriet Mercer was admitted to hospital in immense pain, which was found to be caused by a non-cancerous tumour on her kidney, which had grown to the size of a rugby ball. For the following six weeks Mercer lay in hospital unable to sleep – when she attempted to, she would hallucinate wild visions of gargoyles and demons. Instead, with the transience of existence having been thrown into sharp focus by her near-death experience, Mercer stayed awake, reflecting on the 40 years that had preceded this moment – through the relationships, events and tragedies that had shaped her. From the lonely death of her father to the retrospective processing of sexual abuse, these reflections form the basis of *Gargoyles*. However, far from being simply a memoir about illness and recovery, Mercer's skill is to use this raw subject matter as the basis for a rich literary experiment that evokes the writing of Sinéad Gleeson, in which Mercer explores the relationship between grief, trauma, the body, nature, family, reality, and memory. Accompanied by photography from the author, *Gargoyles* ultimately acts as a philosophical meditation on how to live well. [RG]

How We Might Live **Suzanne Fagence Cooper** (Quercus, £25)

William Morris has always been something of a cultural giant in

HOW WE MIGHT LIVE

At Home with Jane and William Morris

SUZANNE FAGENCE COOPER

Britain. Whether admired for his designs, poetry, or activism, reams of biographical material have been written on the life of the designer who worked at the turn of the 19th century and preoccupied himself with questions of social equality and the reconciliation of modernisation to traditional life.

However in *How We Might Live*, Suzanne Fagence Cooper takes a fresh look at Morris's life by turning her attention to Jane Morris, his wife of almost 40 years. Referring to the pair as Jane and William, the author traces the story of Jane's life, starting with her birth into poverty and then the speed with which she was educated and introduced into cultural life through her engagement to William. Doing away with what she argues are deliberate attempts to play down Jane's influence, Fagence Cooper contends that Jane was equal to

William, and points to their creative collaborations as forces that shaped William's ideas more than anything else. Inviting the reader into the homes and gardens created by the Morrises, *How We Might Live* is an accessible and long overdue look at the life of a woman without whom, the author argues, William Morris's legacy would not be what it is today. [JL]

The Naked Don't Fear the Water
Matthieu Aikins (Fitzcarraldo Editions, £12.99)

Canadian journalist Matthieu Aikins had been working as a foreign reporter in Kabul for several years until 2016, when, with the situation in Afghanistan worsening, his friend Omar – an Afghan translator and driver – decided to flee to Europe. Aikins agreed to accompany Omar on the journey, disguising himself as an Afghan national, and pretending not to be

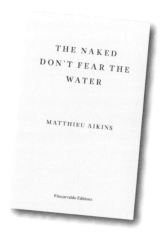

THE NAKED DON'T FEAR THE WATER

MATTHIEU AIKINS

Fitzcarraldo Editions

able to speak English. *The Naked Don't Fear the Water* is Aikins' account of this undercover journey, and offers a rare look into the realities of the people who populate this trail, from refugees, to people smugglers (and why they're so relied on), to the border officials who at one point nearly discover Aikins' true identity. Though the pair are split up several times, Matthieu and Omar travel together from Afghanistan into Iran, then Turkey, and finally to Greece, via refugee camps, precarious inflatable boats, and many overcrowded vehicles. Despite being non-fiction, *The Naked Don't Fear the Water* reads like a novel, with Aikins' skill at depicting dialogue meaning the reader is always gripped by the tension of the present within the book, while also giving voice to the often desperate circumstances of its many displaced characters. [RG]

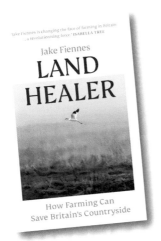

Land Healer: How Farming Can Save Britain's Countryside **Jake Fiennes** (Witness Books, £20)

Opening with a description of bees and dragonflies darting between a hedgerow and wildflowers such as yellow mignonettes, pink mallows, and oxeye daises, it quickly becomes clear that Jake Fiennes' new book *Land Healer* is brimming with knowledge of the earth and its workings. Leafing through the chapters on topics such as how to encourage native bird populations or which plants improve soil quality, it's pleasing to simply read Fiennes' observations of marshes on an early autumn morning or butterflies returning to a pine forest. But as Isabella Tree demonstrates in her description of Fiennes as a "revolutionising force", *Land Healer* contains a compelling argument about how we might regenerate British countryside through farming. Drawing on Fiennes' work as conservation manager at Holkham Estate, *Land Healer* shows that it's possible to address agricultural concerns and restore decimated natural habitats at the same time. When we do so, Fiennes writes, we tackle the climate crisis, public health issues, and create sustainable food supplies for the UK. A vivid, immersive read on vitally important topics. [JL]

For Your Reading Pleasure

As the first Roxy Music album reaches its 50th anniversary, **Will Hodgkinson** *reviews a new book that celebrates the lyrics of Bryan Ferry*

Lyrics **Bryan Ferry**
(Chatto & Windus, £20)

When Tom and I were kids, our parents didn't have a huge record collection. There was the usual selection of boring classical albums stacked in the cabinet next to the solid-state stereo record player with the smoked glass lid. There were the collected works of Cat Stevens, who our father respected as a pop-oriented singer-songwriter because he was "deep"; two Abba albums; and a 45 of "Whispering Grass" by Don Estelle and Windsor Davies, *It Ain't Half Hot Mum* alumni tackling the Ink Spots' sentimental ballad. The records that really did it for us, however, were *For Your Pleasure, Stranded* and *Country Life*, all of them by a band which created a complex and alluring world that our tiny child minds could never hope to understand but were fascinated by anyway: Roxy Music.

First of all there were the album covers. When you're struggling with the reality of actual adult females as sexually attractive beings, the one

lying enticingly in the undergrowth in a ripped red dress, savaged but seductive, on 1973's *Stranded*, was a lot to cope with. The sight of two almost naked German women on 1974's *Country Life*, one covering her bare breasts, the other with a hand over her knickers, both staring impassively at the camera with what seemed like an air of irritation, was confusing to say the least.

Then there was 1973's *For Your Pleasure*, where Bryan Ferry's Amazonian girlfriend Amanda Lear is contorted into a skin-tight black rubber skirt, teetering on sadistically high stilettos as she strains to keep her pet panther on a leash against a city skyline at night, reaching levels of glamour hysteric enough to drive any normal person insane. To venture inside *For Your Pleasure*'s gatefold sleeve was to be assailed by a balding woman in a feather boa (actually Brian Eno at his most flamboyant), a green-haired astronaut in a white space suit (Andy Mackay, saxophone and oboe), a bearded fellow in a matador shirt (Phil Manzanera,

THE
WHITE
REVIEW

'Nothing less than
a cultural revolution'
Deborah Levy

FICTION POETRY ART ESSAYS INTERVIEWS THEWHITEREVIEW.ORG guitar), another man dressed as a woman (Paul Thompson, drummer) and, at the centre, a handsome man who looked like a cross between Elvis Presley and a 1940s matinee idol. This was of course Bryan Ferry, leader of the group, and a man who I would later learn became so consumed by his own creation that he went from art school ironist to upper class arriviste, posing in a white dinner jacket before a swimming pool on the cover of his 1974 solo album *Another Time, Another Place* as he prepared take his place among the establishment he had formerly satirised.

All the members of Roxy Music unquestionably had a part to play, and Eno had such a big part that Ferry couldn't handle it and had to get rid of him, but really Roxy Music is an extension of one man's character. That character reveals itself, for better or for worse, in Bryan Ferry's *Lyrics*.

Being a self-invented person who transformed himself from a Durham farm labourer's son to the kind of chap who refers to himself as "one" with remarkable rapidity, Ferry was always unlikely to spill his heart out in a memoir. As it turns out, *Lyrics* reveals both his genius for filtering romantic visions from films, books and past lives through his own tangled mind, and his ability to find poetic, rather detached ways of expressing the

ennui the gilded life does its best to mask.

Artists and writers are notoriously poor judges of their own work but I was pleased to see, featured on the back of *Lyrics*, the stanza that I have always considered the best thing Ferry ever wrote. "In every dream home a heartache / And every step I take / Takes me further from heaven / Is there a heaven? / I like to think so." Rich in melodrama, pathos and fantasy, not a little ridiculous, it comes from *For Your Pleasure's* "In Every Dream Home a Heartache"; an overwrought ballad that has always struck me as the perfect balance between Ferry's early camp sensibility and his later embrace of luxury and elitism.

Ferry's lecturer at Newcastle was Richard Hamilton, a pop art pioneer who deconstructed Hollywood glamour, the consumer dream and the power of the media in pieces like his 1956 collage of advertising images, *Just What Is it that Makes Today's Homes so Different, so Appealing?*, and 1968's *Swingeing London*, his print of Mick Jagger and the gallery owner Robert Fraser covering their faces as they are arrested for drug charges. "In Every Dream Home A Heartache" was Ferry's attempt to take Hamilton's ideas into a pop song, with a tale of a man falling in love with a rubber doll and facing the agony of futility accordingly. Reaching a crescendo of high drama as Ferry's increasingly feverish delivery captures the torments of a man being driven insane by erotic disaster, it's the ultimate statement of depravity and decadence, delivered in an admirably straight fashion. And only Ferry could offer a preposterous dream of the idealised life like the one featured on "If There Is Something" from the band's 1972 debut album *Roxy Music* – "I would put roses round our door / Sit in our garden / Growing potatoes by the score" – and sing it like his life depended on it.

Funnily enough, in the introduction to *Lyrics* Ferry downplays his own creativity, making it seem less impressive than it actually is. "As Charlie Parker once said, music speaks louder than words," he begins emptily, preparing us for his non-revelations, before explaining how he grew up liking be-bop and Billie Holiday, admired the poetry of Sylvia Plath and TS Eliot, and always loved cinema, so he took these elements into Roxy Music.

For some songs, that straightforward explanation makes sense. Ferry paid homage to Humphrey Bogart in "2HB", from *Roxy Music*, and aped the cleverness of 1930s songwriting greats Cole Porter and Irving Berlin in "Do the Strand", *For Your Pleasure*'s celebration of an imaginary dance that the bright young things of 1970s Britain's Biba-frequenting, *Nova*-reading world are doing. All of it is clever, sophisticated and fun. Ferry's more significant expressions of life as he felt it rather than explained it, however, were yet to come.

As brilliant as "In Every Dream Home A Heartache" is, probably the greatest song Bryan Ferry ever wrote is "Mother of Pearl", from 1973's *Stranded*. Musically it's incredible – it starts out as a frantic nightclub rocker, changes halfway through into a lamenting ballad – but it's the lyrics that stay with you, not least because in them Ferry uncovered the emptiness behind the façade, bringing into question the very purpose of his being in the process. After capturing the thrill of it all (the title of another great Roxy song, incidentally) with words that offer flashes of a wild party – "get the picture", "what's your number", "take a powder" – the mood changes, a plangent piano starts up, and Ferry achieves the remarkable feat of evoking total despair in a way that is funny and touching. There are too many great stanzas in this impressionistic tale of glamour unfolding to repeat here, so I'll just cite my two favourites: "Then I step back thinking of life's inner meaning / And my latest fling," followed not long after by, "If you're looking for love / In a looking glass world / It's pretty hard to find." All delivered in a tragic croon, it makes you think of the sun rising as the party fades, accompanied by the dawning realisation that life's pleasures always fail to compensate for the emptiness that inevitably follows.

When I was younger, I found it disappointing that later Roxy Music albums abandoned pop art playfulness for earnest, aspirational soft rock. With age, I've come to appreciate Ferry's ability to play it straight with a thoughtful, rather mournful take on the romantic song. Even "More Than This", from 1982's *Avalon*, on the face of it the ultimate example of what has since become defined as yacht rock, contains unfathomed sadness. "You know there's nothing / More than this" could be taken as a celebration of a moment shared by two people, but it could also be an acceptance of life's limitations and the fact that whatever you have, whoever you are with and whatever you have achieved will only go so far toward the attainment of happiness.

"Slave to Love" lacks the dazzling wordplay of early Roxy, but when Ferry croons, "Tell her I'll be waiting / In the usual place / With the tired and weary / And there's no escape," you don't feel for a minute that getting all the things he thought he wanted has led to complacency or contentment. In fact, for all of his impeccable dress sense, Gatsby-esque reinvention, and desire to set himself apart from

normal people and his normal background through success, wealth and fame, Ferry has never come across as a man with a satisfied mind. Perhaps that's why, whether he's singing about falling in love with a blow-up doll or a beautiful woman like Jerry Hall, Bryan Ferry cannot help but evoke poetic decadence, despite his best efforts at just being another normal, stately home-dwelling, gentlemen's club-visiting, fox hunting sons-siring member of the establishment. 🐌

Lyrics by Bryan Ferry is out now. Will Hodgkinson's In Perfect Harmony: Singalong Pop In 70s Britain *will be published by Nine Eight Books in September.*

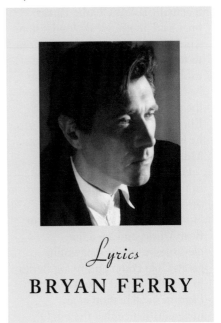

Lyrics
BRYAN FERRY

Books in Brief
Further reading

A concise round-up of essential idler reading, by **Julia Lasica**

The Trespasser's Companion
Nick Hayes
(Bloomsbury, £14.99)
How can we reconnect with the world around us when 92 per cent of England is private property? How can we reclaim our right to the land when 97 per cent of English rivers are privately owned? In this comprehensive guide to trespassing, bestselling writer Nick Hayes outlines practical steps we can take to answer those burning questions. Packed full of beautiful woodcuts and testimonies from radical ramblers.

Smoke Hole: Looking to the Wild in the Time of the Spyglass
Martin Shaw (Chelsea Green, £14.99)
From the celebrated mythologist and wilderness guide Martin Shaw, this book guides the reader in using tales to navigate modern life. 'Shaw encourages and illuminates the mythic in our own lives. He is a modern day bard', said Madeline

Miller, author of Circe and The Song of Achilles. As Shaw himself writes, 'May you set out on the most magnificent journey' after reading this book.

Overland: Travelling with No Plan
Richard Kaufmann, translated by **Rachel Ward** (REH, €23.36)
With a forward from *Idler* editor Tom Hodgkinson, *Overland* embraces train travel in Europe in true Idler style. With colourful illustrations and a pull-out rail map, these accounts of trains and travel – from sleeping in bunks on a trundling train to goal-less summer journeys – will make you want to book a ticket and roam.

THE PHYSICK GARDEN

Ancient Cures for Modern Maladies

A book of surrealist illustrations exploring tales of medicinal plants

ALICE SMITH

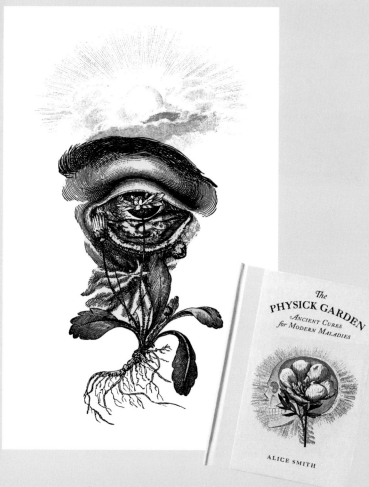

Frances Lincoln Publishers Ltd
ISBN 9780711266339
£16.00

FRANCES
LINCOLN

Drawn to Nature: Gilbert White and the Artists **Simon Martin**
(Pallant House Gallery Trust, £25)

Opening with an introduction by David Attenborough on Gilbert White's life, this book maps the various ways in which artists and writers such as Eric Ravilious, John Piper, Virginia Woolf and WH Auden responded to the celebrated naturalist's works. Overflowing with beautiful images, Simon Martin's study proves the enduring relevance of White's work today.

Delphi **Clare Pollard**
(Fig Tree, £12.99, out 28 July)

Described by award-winning author Evie Wyld as "a compact miracle of a book", *Idler* poetry editor Clare Pollard's first novel is a thought-provoking mirror to modern society. Set in lockdown 2020, it follows the life of a married mother whose life is punctured by contemporary upheavals. But the past also enters her life – oracles, divinations, tarot cards – propelling her to an uncertain future…

Portable Magic: A History of Books and their Readers **Emma Smith**
(Allen Lane, £20)

Taking Stephen King's assertion that all books are "a uniquely portable magic", Professor of Shakespeare Studies Emma Smith leads us through the millennium-long story of the book, focusing on the physical objects themselves, and the spells they cast over us. "I lost count of the times I exclaimed with delight when I read a nugget of information I hadn't encountered before," wrote Val McDermid for the *Times*.

Careering **Daisy Buchanan**
(Little, Brown Book Group, £14.99)

Writer and broadcaster Daisy Buchanan's second novel is a hilarious dark comedy addressing the classic dilemma we find ourselves in when we realise our jobs don't love us back. "Quite simply the funniest novel I've read all year," said author and journalist Nell Frizzell. 🐞

Our interviews with Nick Hayes, Emma Smith and Daisy Buchanan for A Drink with the Idler can be seen by Idler members at idler.co.uk

Music
Ghosts in the Machine

Stewart Lee *creaks opens the radiophonic*
vaults and lets the sonic spirits fly

H WÆT! FORGOTTEN MICRO-
MOVEMENT suddenly
declared scene of significance!
Captured Tracks' compilation
Strum & Thrum: The American
Jangle Underground 1983–1987
critically reappraises the eyeblink
before propulsive trebly American
indie-pop became an off-the-peg
stylistic option, crack-trapped at the
death of vinyl and the birth of CD.
The Primitons' "All My Friends" is
the Byrds pogoing on the spot; 28th
Day's raggedly transcendental
"Pages Turn" is both infinite and
claustrophobic; Absolute Grey are
Jefferson Airplane in a broom
cupboard with perpetual

nervousness. A skint, skinny me sold
off slabs of this stuff. Bollocks. Who
knew it was tomorrow's *Nuggets*?

Vic Godard's value was always
obvious, his short-lived punk-era
flâneurs Subway Sect eschewing
Seventies snottiness for a shabby-
chic bohemia that shaped the
bookish eighties anti-rock of
Postcard, Creation and C86.
Produced by The Clash's Mick
Jones, they're back with *Moments
Like These*, a suave Roxy survivors'
Buena Vista Social Club, spicing
garage rock'n'roll with showtune
surges, ratpack bonhomie, and
Cuban rhythms. The album unrolls
like an evening out, Godard your

guide round a circuit of swinging dives, swigging small sour drinks as his almost-crooned vocals grow ever more appropriate, neither withered by age nor condemned by the years.

The Ghost Box label assiduously channels sounds derived from seventies children's TV and public information films, seemingly more sinister as memory decomposes. But the debut from former Wolf People frontman Jack Sharp's Large Plants is a stylistic departure, implying the organic soundtrack of a New English Library-hued horror-biker trash-flick that never was. *The Carrier* sees undercover Operation Julie officers close in, as cowbell-clattering proto-metal bleeds into the fading funereal flowers of folk rock; a bastard sound that didn't quite exist, but should have done because it's ace.

Paddy Considine, our greatest living thespian, has surgical focus. His early Riding the Low releases method-acted the precision

techniques of his inspiration, Guided By Voices' Robert Pollard, as if Rock Star were a role. But on the group's third album, *The Death of Gobshite Rambo*, RTL deploy Pollard's economy and in-the-moment intensity to find their own pulsating power-pop prog-punk identity, Considine knowing instinctively where to vacate a vowel or cluck a consonant. The gravitational pull of influence escaped, we indulge the lone GBV-alike, "By-Product of the Last Flats", and embrace it.

What is authenticity anyway? Tanya Tagaq ain't your standard World Music stash, and the Canadian Inuk musician combines traditional throat singing techniques with filthy electronica, in an increasingly anguished howl at the historic abuse of First Nations. You may have to squint to discern the visceral physicality of Tagaq's retched and wrenched growls and proclamations, as she and

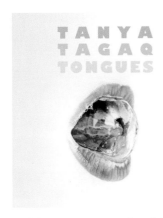

collaborators Gonjasufi and Saul Williams have somewhat smothered these al fresco expulsions with serrated swathes of electronics, but *Tongues* remains vitally uneasy listening.

Acoustic guitarist Glenn Jones sounds authentic, but the American Primitive style of action-fingerpicking he adopted was a construction of fifties blues freak John Fahey who, in the guise of Blind Joe Death, applied the mind-expanding dynamics of the incoming age to traditional forms

and inadvertently spawned a school. In his shadow, Jones ekes unexpected depth out of artisanal tunes, but gradually his tenth solo album, *Vade Mecum*, spins you into a spatial six-string stratosphere of brain-dilating bent. I elect to remember seeing Jones play in a Seattle bar sometime soon after the millennium, but in reality everything's a blur and I'm essentially choosing my own adventures now.

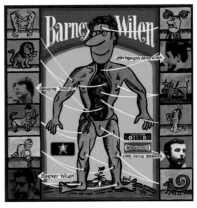

In Britain and Holland experimental sixties jazzers such as The Spontaneous Music Ensemble or the Instant Composers Pool sought their own voices, distinct from the African-American accent. But the French saxophonist Barney Wilen blew on Miles Davis's soundtrack to Louis Malle's *Ascenseur Pour l'Échafaud*, and this reissue of his 1966 *Zodiac* album initially suggests a spirited Rive Gauche retread of contemporary American jazz. Then, halfway through, the clattering carillon of bell-like percussion on "Balance" ushers in the non-idiomatic moves of Wilen's fellow Europeans and *Zodiac* becomes a fertile cultural cross-fuck.

Why worry where Wilen waits on the time/originality axis? Today's kids absorb all music simultaneously, and 1966's *Zodiac* could probably accommodate much of Broadcast's 2003 *Microtronics Volumes 01 & 02*, French jazz interrupted by gas-fired radiophonics. One of three new

archival releases, it further evidences the quiet genius of Birmingham's electrodelica pioneers. *Maida Vale Sessions* is the most accessible, BBC Radio dry runs of time-travelling dreamy domestic science pop ballads, the late Trish Keenan, as Delia Derbyshire with the head of Françoise Hardy, smoking shit fags on the set of *Abigail's Party*. A generation's idea of how the past thought the future would sound starts here. Suddenly, drunkenly, I am sincerely sad for someone I never knew. Forward!

The bodily atoms of Hawkwind's sole remaining original member, 80-year-old Dave Brock, will have been entirely replaced since the group formed in 1969, but today they have never sounded more like their classic seventies steamroller-to-the-stars incarnation. The Hawkwind that fans treasure probably isn't the one captured on this bold three-CD set,

Dreamworkers of Time: The BBC Recordings 1985–1995. Eighties Hawkwind were inappropriately adopted by the New Wave of British Heavy Metal, and they subsequently enjoyed a symbiotic relationship with the nineties crusty rave scene, which gained cultural validation by association. A 1986 live set from Reading sees Lemmy return to ride an 11-minute, but fat-free, "Silver Machine", while in a 1995 radio session the rave Hawkwind deliver a punkish version of the still canonical Travellers' protest anthem "The Right to Decide". But I, having had my coordinates fully scrambled at the London Palladium last October, declare today's Hawkwind definitive, whoever's actually on stage. So what does that mean?

Wet Leg's joint ages add up to less than Dave Brock's, and their freshers' floor-filler "Wet Dream", along with the immorally moreish "Chaise Longue", were lockdown's wittiest earworms. The polished post-punk pop of the waspish Isle of Wight bonnet-wearers' eponymous debut encouragingly suggests escape routes from the primrose prison of popularity and expectation. I, of course, saw the first Pixies/Throwing Muses tour, Blake Babies at the Borderline, and The Breeders' live debut, so I affect indifference to this latest iteration. And yet here I stand, ecstatically immobilised before Wet Leg, sounding like they just quit college in Boston circa 1989. And I'm Gustav von Aschenbach choking to death in Venice, waves of bouncing boys breaking on the Brixton Academy beach beside me, my reservations about provenance washed away. Wet Leg teach me that I am mortal. But life will go on. Altogether now! "On the chaise longue, on the chaise longue, on the chaise longue, all day long, on the chaise longue! John Barleycorn must die!" 🍏

Strum & Thrum: The American Jangle Underground 1983–1987
  (Captured Tracks)
Subway Sect *Moments Like These* (Texte und Töne)
Large Plants *The Carrier* (Ghost Box)
Riding the Low *The Death of Gobshite Rambo* (Clinical Finish)
Tanya Tagaq *Tongues* (Six Shooter)
Glenn Jones *Vade Mecum* (Thrill Jockey)
Barney Wilen *Zodiac* (We Are Busy Bodies)
Broadcast *Microtronics Volumes 01 & 02; Mother Is the Milky Way;*
  Maida Vale Sessions (Warp)
Hawkwind *Dreamworkers of Time: The BBC Recordings 1985–1995*
  (Atomhenge)
Wet Leg *Wet Leg* (Domino)

"THE PAPER IS JAMMING AGAIN"

Television
Game Changer

*Peter Fincham on that peculiar niche of television presentation,
the unexpected quiz show host*

LATER THIS YEAR Richard Osman, the lanky daytime TV host and best-selling crime novelist, is leaving *Pointless* in order to concentrate on his writing. Many writers, of course, spend their days watching daytime television and thinking, "Why did I decide to start writing in the first place? Wouldn't it be a lot easier to present an undemanding quiz like *Pointless*? Better paid, too." But Richard is passing them in the opposite direction. You might have done the same if the advance you got for your next book was equal to the GDP of a small South American country.

This is the latest twist in the dazzling ascent of Richard Osman. Not long ago he was a producer at the international production conglomerate Endemol. I have happy memories of him coming to see me with his creative partner Tim Hincks, pitching ideas not unlike *Pointless*. I was a channel controller at the time, at the BBC and then ITV, and they were hungry for commissions. (Full disclosure: Tim Hincks is now my partner in our production company Expectation. People say that television is a "chumocracy", but where's the evidence?)

Osman was always amusing and had smart ideas, but it never occurred to me that he had the qualities to become a TV presenter himself. There's something pleasingly random about the moment his life changed. The format for *Pointless* was being pitched to the BBC. In the absence of a seasoned professional to play the part of the "other" presenter, Richard stepped in. He did it so well he was offered the role on the spot and a star was born.

Many ideas like *Pointless* are pitched to broadcasters. They are the acorns that litter the forest floor of television; very few grow into mighty oaks. It follows that many producers in run-throughs play the parts later offered to the likes of Claudia Winkleman or Bradley Walsh. These pitches take place in draughty meeting rooms where trestle tables stand in for shiny sets and questions are written on revision cards. Afterwards, everyone goes back to their open-plan desks, grabbing something from Pret a Manger on the way.

So what was it about Richard Osman? I wasn't there, but I can confidently say there is no science whatsoever in making these sorts of life-changing decisions. Somebody just had a hunch. He has a lugubrious tone and a distinctive look. He seems brainy. He hadn't been in front of a camera before, but once he got his break it became clear that, to use a phrase, the camera liked him. What does that mean? Nobody really knows.

Television is full of unlikely stories like this. Denis Norden met his comedy-writing partner Frank Muir in 1947. They toiled away on innumerable radio and television series before someone at ITV came up with the idea of putting together an occasional show of outtakes and bloopers. The programme was called *It'll Be Alright On The Night*. It launched on 18 September 1977 and was watched by – wait for it – 16.45 million people. Denis Norden became an overnight star, 30 years after he'd begun.

Similarly, the presenter William G Stewart started working in television in 1965. He had previously had an unusual career, first as a Butlin's redcoat and later as the private secretary to the Labour MP Tom Driberg. In the late 1980s, having produced countless series

behind the camera, he bought the format for an idea originally called *Twenty to One*. He paid £200 for it – the best £200 he ever spent, as he subsequently said to anyone who interviewed him. He renamed the format *Fifteen to One* and sold it to Channel 4. Various presenters were considered, including Jonathan Ross and John Stapleton, before Stewart decided he might as well take on the role himself. It ran for over 2,000 episodes.

Maybe most of us, if opportunity knocked, would grab the chance to host a television programme. Maybe every researcher who reads in for a famous presenter in a draughty meeting room is secretly waiting for the tap on the shoulder.

All the benefits that flow from that moment – interviews, publicists, commercials, flattery, decent tables in fashionable restaurants, after-dinner speeches, costume assistants, agents who negotiate eye-watering fees, publishers who wonder if you've ever thought of writing a novel – sound like a recipe for happiness to most of us. It's as if, having spent a lifetime turning right on the plane, someone says, "From now on, turn left, and we'll pay you generously to do so."

Whether that actually constitutes happiness is beyond the scope of this article. But it seems to be working out pretty well for Richard Osman. ☻

IDLE PURSUITS

Gardening
Liquid Asset

When the summer heat leaves your garden parched,
it's tempting to turn on the hose and get spraying.
But there are eco-friendlier ways to keep everything looking rosy.
Graham Burnett *is overflowing with ideas*

IF SOIL IS the skin of this small planet we inhabit, then water is surely its lifeblood, upon which all of its ecosystems depend. Over 70 per cent of the Earth's surface is covered by oceans, yet the fresh water essential for our food production accounts for less than three per cent of the world's total, and of this the major part is inaccessible, locked up in deep aquifers and glaciers.

One in nine people in the world lack access to safe drinking water, while annual rainfall continues to decline worldwide due to climate change, and desertification is inexorably spreading as forests are cleared for cattle, or for the production of soy or grain.

Such global challenges may seem abstract, yet summer is when we gardeners and allotmenteers are acutely aware of water scarcity as clay soils become parched and cracked, lawns turn brown and hose pipe bans come into play. The conservation of this precious resource is the responsibility of all of us, and by adopting a few permaculture and water harvesting principles on our own plots we can all think globally while acting locally.

Observation Is Key
Use all your senses to see where water flows and how it behaves on your site. What type of soil do you have? What wild plants or weeds are thriving and what can they tell you? Observe over a number of seasons. My allotment is situated next to a natural spring surrounded by moisture-loving willow. It gets waterlogged and even flooded most winters, but when the water table drops in summer it's as dry as a bone.

Catch and Store Water
Fitting butts for harvesting at least some of the 100,000 litres or so of the rainwater that annually falls onto our roofs is a no-brainer – it's a simple intervention and can drastically reduce your reliance on mains water, particularly if you have the space to connect a few together in series. Installing a pond not only gives you water storage, it can have other uses too, such as providing an oasis where birds and hedgehogs will come to drink, and attracting frogs and toads, which offer natural pest control.

Slow it, Spread it, Sink it
Rather than having water erosively run off your land, encourage it to stick around and infiltrate the soil by adopting no-dig or low-tillage practices. Covering bare ground with mulches such as cardboard, woodchip or organically sourced straw to prevents evaporation, while adding plenty of organic matter such as well-rotted compost, will increase the water-retaining capacity of the soil as well as feeding and stimulating the soil food web of earthworms, mycorrhizal fungi, bacteria and other beneficial microorganisms.

Reduce, Reuse, Recycle
A sustainable system is about making use of resources as often as possible between entering and leaving that system. It makes sense for household water to be graded so that as it deteriorates in quality it can be used appropriately. For example "grey" water (from the bath or washing up bowl) could be reused to water your garden plants during dry periods rather than sending it straight down the plughole and into the sewers. You could even consider installing a compost toilet. Otherwise, discarded two-litre plastic soda bottles can be recycled into a simple irrigation system. Cut off the bottom, remove the lid, turn upside down and half bury in soil surrounded by two or three newly planted seedlings.

Filling the bottle with water will ensure diffusion into the surrounding soil and encourage deeper rooting of young plants.

Timing Is Everything

If you must cultivate, do so as early in the year as possible (but not when the soil is still wet and its structure easily damaged – February is probably too early, March is ideal). Cultivating soils after the beginning of April is more likely to cause severe moisture loss. After this it's better to loosen any compaction by wiggling a fork into the ground or lightly surface-hoeing off any weeds rather than turning the soil over. Sowing early, before May where possible, will allow crops to root into moist soil before severe drought arrives. Later sowings from June onwards might have to be made into dry soil. Where this is the case, a water-efficient way of ensuring good germination is to apply water along the drill (the groove cut in the soil) before sowing.

Practice Correct Placement

Get the plants right for your situation. If growing annual crops, choose ones that are appropriate for your soil conditions and locality. Root crops like carrots, beetroot, parsnips and turnips are fairly drought-tolerant. Salad and other leafy vegetables such as spinach are less so, although chard is pretty

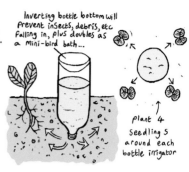

PLASTIC BOTTLE IRRIGATOR
Cut bottom off of a 2 litre plastic bottle. Remove lid and half bury in soil. Filling bottle with water will ensure diffusion into surrounding soil and encourage deeper rooting of seedlings than surface watering.

Inverting bottle bottom will prevent insects, debris, etc falling in, plus doubles as a mini-bird bath...

plant 4 seedling s around each bottle irrigator

resilient (a relative of beetroot, it has a deep rooting system). Plants that set fruit, or pods such as peas, beans, tomatoes or peppers, are most vulnerable at flowering time. While a permaculture approach is generally fairly tolerant of so-called "weeds", such plants can compete for water and nutrients, so consider keeping them well controlled if you hope for a reasonable yield.

Think Generations Ahead

Plan for the longer term. Established permanent crops are less susceptible to drought, and devoting a larger proportion of your plot to soft fruit, rhubarb and globe artichokes for example, is worth considering. Transitioning from annual cropping to forest gardening systems that combine fruit trees, fruit bushes and perennial veggies that are largely self-maintaining once established might also make sense as climate change inevitably makes its mark on how we feed ourselves. ⊚

Beekeeping

Chemical Romance

Bill Anderson *on how bees deliver the spark of attraction*
between plants that keep them growing anew

NOTHING COMES AS close to
defining the idle beekeeper as
reclining in front of a midsummer
hive, mesmerised by the buzzing
industry of the worker bees. They
seamlessly shoot out of the entrance
to forage for food, elegantly avoided
by sister aeronauts floating home
laden with their own gaudy pellets
of pollen latched to their legs, and
their abdomens invisibly full of
freshly gathered nectar.

Edge closer and you'll be stopped
in your tracks. The scent of
countless blossoms' nectar being
busily distilled down to honey wafts
from the hive entrance, dissolving
time. In the dark interior bees are
storing the summer sunlight you
feel on your skin as syrupy sweetness
to sustain them through the winter
that will come. But this fragrant
honey won't just survive this winter
– it will keep its sunlight
indefinitely, a timescale beyond
measure, an aroma-beguiling
meditation.

The pollen that is carefully
packed into tiny baskets of hair on
the bees' back legs has come from

flowers as far away as three miles.
When the bees visit a bloom to
gather as many of these protein-
packed grains as quickly as they can,
they not only carry pollen from
previously visited flowers, they also
carry a significant positive charge of
static electricity generated by the
beating of their wings. When they
land, that static is discharged, and
loose grains on the bee's body fly off
onto the plant like sparks of
attraction. The lucky pollen grains
from afar that land on the surface of
the stigma of the plant are instantly
subjected to a chemical
interrogation by the plant consisting
of three key questions:

1. "Are you my species?" Because,
   like us, they prefer their tall, dark
   strangers not too strange. If the
   answer is yes…

2. "Are you me?" Just like us,
   romance with a mirror has its
   limitations. If the answer is no,
   then it's…

3. "You're gorgeous – shall we
   mate?"

   The pollen grain obliges with a
   single cell which forms a tube that

penetrates the stigma and heads down its length towards the plant's ovary. In some species of corn this requires a 12-inch tube and takes 24 hours – phenomenal growth from a grain the size of a speck of dust. In most flowers, however, the magic is shorter and quicker, and as soon as the pollen tube reaches the ovary, the male sperm from the grain begin to flow through it and the offspring of the plant are begun.

Honeybees are particularly good at reliably delivering pollen grains to plants that get past that first "Are you my species?" question because on a given foraging flight they will only visit plants of the same species – great for the plant's sex life, but also very practical for the bees: they discovered they could pack more grains into their pollen baskets if they are all of the same species with a uniform size and shape.

None of the grains in the pollen pellets you see being flown into the hive will ever get to grow their

inseminating insertion, but the extraordinary density of protein required to generate that growth will now be used to nourish baby bees – who will in time return to other flowers to deliver the pollen they need to conceive their children, in exchange for surplus pollen and nectar. And if the bees generate surplus honey, we can share in this scented sweetness of summer symbiosis.

IDLER FESTIVAL

8–10 July 2022 | Fenton House, Hampstead

JARVIS COCKER

SALLY PHILLIPS · ARTHUR SMITH

GLEN BAXTER · MARGARET DRABBLE · GAVIN TURK

LAUREN CHILD · ELIF SHAFAK · LEA YPI

TOM HODGKINSON · AKASH KAPUR &

WILLIAM DALRYMPLE · NELL HUDSON

JOHN LLOYD · SARAH JAFFE · GUY STANDING

DAISY BUCHANAN · VIRGINIA IRONSIDE · DAVID WENGROW

CRISPIN HUNT & WILL HODGKINSON · HANNAH DAWSON

LUCY COOKE · BEN MOOR · ROWAN PELLING · MATTHEW GREEN

"The combination of Idler and Fenton House is irresistible; where better to open the floodgates of reflection?"
MICHAEL PALIN

National Trust

FRIDAY 8 JULY

Surrealist Walk *with* Arthur Smith

What is TV for? *with* Sally Phillips, John Lloyd and Peter Fincham

Against Careering *with* Daisy Buchanan

The Problem with Interest *with* Edward Chancellor

Reviving the Commons *with* Guy Standing

Sex Robots *with* Kate Devlin

Louis Eliot

Ask the Agony Aunt

Workshops with the Idler Tutors

SATURDAY 9 JULY

Jarvis Cocker in Conversation *with* Tom Hodgkinson

Sally Phillips

Akash Kapur in Conversation *with* William Dalrymple

Ben Moor: Who Here's Lost?

What Does it Mean to Be Free? *with* Lea Ypi

David Wengrow in Conversation *with* Mark Vernon

Getting Medieval *with* Seb Falk and Mary Wellesley

A Midsummer Mooch through Moominland Midwinter *with* David Bramwell

The Best of Indie Publishing *with* Makina Books, Peninsula Press & Prototype Publishing

Nonsense Poetry *with* Clare Pollard

How to Holiday Greener *with* Richard Hammond

Insect Talk and Walk with Bridget Nicholls

Release Your Inner Cartoonist *with* Harry Venning

A Walk in Georgian Hampstead *with* Harry Mount

Glasses through Time *with* Travis Elborough

Ask the Agony Aunt

Workshops with the Idler Tutors

Afterparty at the Hampstead Jazz Club Featuring Fraülein, Thrill City and more

SUNDAY 10 JULY

Lauren Child in Conversation *with* Tom Hodgkinson

Elif Shafak

Fix Streaming Now *with* Crispin Hunt and Will Hodgkinson

Margaret Drabble in Conversation *with* Tom Hodgkinson

The Future of Work *with* Sarah Jaffe, Brendan Burchell and Amelia Horgan

Glen Baxter

Nell Hudson in Conversation *with* Florence Read

The Truth about Female Animals *with* Lucy Cooke

Warszawa Wschodnia

Lost Cities of Britain *with* Matthew Green

Philosophy Walk *with* Mark Vernon

Midori Jaeger

The Radical Life and Legacy of Mary Wollstonecraft *with* Hannah Dawson and Amelia Horgan

Singalong *with* Charles Hazlewood

Impro for Writers *with* John-Paul Flintoff

A Walk round Literary Hampstead *with* Henry Eliot

Bibliotherapy *with* Ella Berthoud

Make Your Own Manifesto Zine

Wild Food *with* Lucia Stuart

ALL WEEKEND

The Art Car Boot Fair. *Hip hop dancing on the lawn with Oliver Broadbent of the Mudflappers*; Chill Out Tent in the attic; *wandering minstrels in the garden*; harpsichord recitals in the house; *silent disco in the rose garden*; stalls from fabulous independent businesses; *the Idler bookshop*; delicious food from Café Tangerine; *cocktails in the orchard*; and many more surprises.

VENUES:

Fenton House
cared for by the National Trust
Hampstead Grove London NW3 6SP
Timings: 18:00–21:00 on Friday,
12:00–19:00 on Saturday and Sunday

The Hampstead Jazz Club at
The Duke of Hamilton,
23–25 New End Hampstead
London NW3 1JD
Timings: 19:00–23:00 on Saturday

Tickets: £40–£125

To book: idler.co.uk

PROGRAMME SUBJECT TO CHANGE

Sheds

Amazing Glazing

Alex Johnson finds a summerhouse in Staffordshire whose stunning stained glass designs cast a whole new light on the sheddie-sphere

AS THE 19TH CENTURY politician, abolitionist, and educator Horace Mann once very nearly said, a house without books is like a shed without windows. But not all windows are made the same, and after 16 years of writing about backyard bolt-holes, I think I've found my favourite shed fenestration…

The Apothecary's Den started life as a rundown summerhouse, painted an unsightly bright blue and with broken windows. It was spotted at a shed supplier in Staffordshire by Rachel Carpenter, who bought and repainted it, hooked it up with electricity, and added personal interior touches, including curtains and a lampshade decorated with her four favourite garden moths using a Tiffany technique. She also re-glazed it with stained glass, the images depicting plants used in medicine.

"For a long time, the idea behind it had been sitting in my head," she says. "As a community pharmacist for more than 30 years, I can remember vividly the lectures I had detailing the plants that give us *materia medica*, or the substances that we used – and in some cases still use – in medicine. As I've got older, I've become more interested in the relationship between our health and the natural world. Depicting this in a meaningful design became a bit of an obsession and when I saw there was a night school class for stained glass beginners at my local college, I had no hesitation in giving it a go. Little did I know the project would actually come to fruition in a summerhouse, despite having no glazing experience, and that it would take five years to finish."

That beginners' class bore considerable fruit. The results are beautiful – six large handmade stained glass windows that flood the Den with light, as well as making it visually appealing from inside and out. ((Search "the apothecary's den" on YouTube.) The window in the door focuses on echinacea (a traditional herbal remedy) and atropa belladonna, aka deadly nightshade, which is poisonous but

Light bulb moment:
the Apothecary's Den
looks stunning
lit up at night

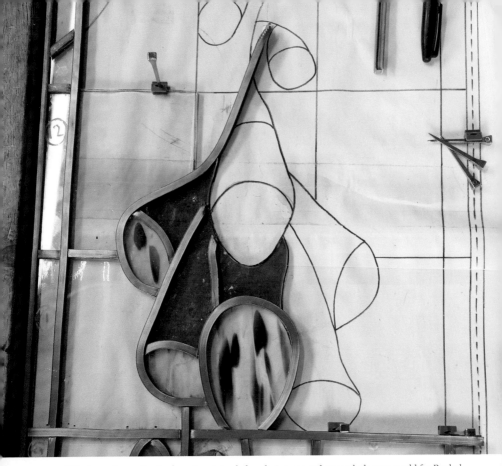

Windows of opportunity: learning stained glass design opened up a whole new world for Rachel

also contains atropine, used to dilate the pupils. It also includes a house sparrow, one of the few birds that visits Rachel's urban garden.

Then there's the window dedicated to chamomile and its soothing properties, as well as the ergot fungus that used to be taken, in carefully controlled measures, to deal with migraines. The others present us with a willow (whose bark gives us aspirin), snowdrops (galantamine for use against dementia), a poppy (morphine) and a host of nocturnal mammals, including a badger, bat and fox.

"Learning the techniques of stained glass was also a way to switch off from work and make new friends," explains Rachel. "And there's always something new to learn or some problem to solve. In designing a leaded window, each piece of glass must be cut to shape, so the shapes can't be too intricate or unstable. Then each shape has to be surrounded by a thin channel of lead to make it secure in its place.

Finally everything is soldered together and sealed to be weatherproof.

"The designs for all six windows probably took longer to draw than the manufacturing process itself. My inexperience possibly led me to be over-ambitious in some of the tiny pieces I incorporated, especially in the willow window. Occasionally I realised the design I'd drawn wasn't going to work visually. I changed the position of the bat in the gothic window when I was almost finished so that it appeared on the other side. As I look back now with more experience, I can see where I would make changes given another chance but in general I'm really pleased with how the Den has come together."

Finally, Rachel offers *Idler* readers a nature challenge. "The Den windows feature ten plants. Nine of them are described on Instagram @ theapothecarysden. Can you work out what the tenth is?" 🐌

Alex Johnson runs Shedworking (shedworking.co.uk). His latest book is Rooms of Their Own: Where Great Writers Write.

Making an entrance: the door design features echinacea flowers, deadly nightshade and a sparrow

Travel

Get on Board

A guide to paddle-boarding in Britain and Europe by Green Traveller writer **Richard Hammond**

ONE OF THE advantages of paddle-boarding over some of the other kit-heavy watersports is that you can use inflatable paddle boards that can be packed away into a small bag and carried on public transport to reach some wonderful locations.

Many waterways in England and Wales require a licence to paddle. You can buy an annual one as part of membership of British Canoeing (britishcanoeing.org.uk) or you can buy a specific licence for the waterways managed by the Canal & River Trust (canalrivertrust.org.uk), the Environment Agency (gov.uk), and the Broads Authority for paddling in the Norfolk Broads (broads-authority.gov.uk).

In Scotland there's the "right to roam" so you don't require a licence, but joining the Scottish Canoe Association will give you lots of information about routes, access, courses and clubs. Here are some great locations for paddle-boarding that can easily be reached by public transport.

1. The coastline of Swansea Bay and the Gower Peninsula is blessed with a wonderful range of rivers, estuaries, streams, points, reefs and beaches that are easily reached by bus from Swansea (swanseabaywithoutacar.co.uk). Stand Up Paddle Gower hires out boards and runs lessons for all levels at over 20 locations throughout the Gower, as well as a night-time Glow Paddle in the more sheltered area at Mumbles (supgower.com).

2. The Trent in the Midlands is the third-longest river in the UK (after the Thames and Severn) and is great for a day out or longer paddle-touring multi-day adventure. The river was a transport highway during the 19th century, rising in the Staffordshire moors and meandering through large industrial cities, including Stoke-on-Trent and Nottingham before joining the River Ouse and entering the North Sea via the Humber estuary. Along the way, it passes under the mediaeval bridge

Ducking not diving: a paddle-boarder negotiates tricky waters in Cornwall

at Swarkestone, by Newark Castle and some wonderful sprawling countryside. Calm Yoga SUP School runs a wide range of beginner and improver courses and sessions as well as SUP Yoga from its base in Burton upon Trent (calm.online).

3. Frenchman's Creek is a peaceful picturesque inlet off the Helford River just south of Falmouth.

Koru Kayaking runs guided paddle-boarding tours from Helford Passage across to the creek – the inspiration for Daphne du Maurier's novel *Frenchman's Creek* – along banks of ancient oaks. Beginners can go to the nearby, and more sheltered, Port Navas Creek with beautiful river-fronted houses and magical wooded smaller creeks, while more experienced paddlers can try several secluded beaches and caves near Durgan, depending on wind direction and tides (korukayaking.co.uk). The Line 35 bus runs from Falmouth to Helford Passage (firstbus.co.uk).

4. Lulworth Cove is a beautiful shell-shaped oasis on the Jurassic Coast in West Dorset from where you can paddle along the World Heritage coast to the natural arch of Durdle Door – out on the open sea, you're far from the masses that can crowd this famous natural attraction, and it's a wonderful paddle along the coast, with views of the spectacular white limestone cliffs and golden shingle beaches. Lulworth Activities is based at a hotel built in the 1650s on the shores of Lulworth Cove and hires boards by the hour or for a full day (lulworth-activities.co.uk). The X54 Weymouth-Poole bus runs via Lulworth Cove and the Durdle Door park entrance (firstbus.co.uk).

5. The River Arun in West Sussex has one of the strongest tides in the UK and is a wonderful paddle from Littlehampton inland to Arundel, with views of the spectacular 11th-century Arundel Castle and the South Downs, while the upper stretch travels through the Arundel Wetland Centre to end at the Riverside Tea Rooms in Amberley (riversidesouthdowns.com). You can also hire stand-up paddle boards from here. There are several operators that run paddle-boarding trips along the Arun, including Moxie Unleashed (moxieunleashed.com) and TJ Board Hire (tjboardhire.co.uk). There's a railway station in Arundel with rail connections from London, and it's also the bus stop for several local bus services throughout West Sussex and beyond.

6. The River Dee runs through beautiful Royal Deeside from its source high in the Cairngorm mountains for 88 miles (142km) passing mountains, moorland, pine forest, birchwood and farmland, as well as several small towns and villages, on its way to the sea at Aberdeen harbour. Stonehaven Paddleboarding runs guided trips – from three hours up to a full day – along the Dee from Stonehaven, where there's a railway station with rail connections to Aberdeen and Edinburgh (shpb.co.uk).

More Info
A nationwide initiative from British Canoeing Go Paddling encourages people to go canoeing, kayaking and stand-up paddle-boarding. Its website lists hundreds of paddle

points and slipways throughout the UK in rivers, lakes and canals, and provides links to paddle operators, kit hire, centres and clubs (gopaddling.info).

Paddle-Boarding in Europe

1. Those who've honed their paddle-boarding skills will love this twilight paddle-boarding trip along the banks of the Upper Tarn Valley in southwest France. From Trébas Leisure Centre, you'll set off at dusk on summer evenings with local expert Charly for a 7km adventure passing rock walls, small villages and lots of wildlife – there's an emphasis on trying to see beavers in the moonlight (tourisme-tarn.com). Bus 202 runs from Albi to Trébas (it takes about 50 minutes).

2. Lac de Clarens in the heart of the Lot-et-Garonne region of France is a great place to combine spending a few hours paddle-boarding then exploring the nearby forest. The outdoor activity centre Castel Adventure (casteladventure.com) provides boards if you don't have your own, as well as canoes and pedal boats. There's a train station at Lac de Clarens with connections from Bergerac and Marmande via Casteljaloux.

3. Explore Zurich from its waterways. A three-hour guided tour provides instruction for paddle-boarding beginners while you also learn about the history of this city. If you're there for a few days, it's worth buying the city travel pass, which gives you unlimited travel by tram, bus, train, boat and cable car throughout the city and the surrounding region, as well as free or reduced admission to over 40 museums. The paddle-boarding tour departs from Strandbad Mythenquai, just a few minutes' walk from the bus stop at Sukkulentensammlung.

4. Make the most of Eurostar's new daily direct train from London to Amsterdam (it's just under four hours), then explore the Amstel river and canals on your paddleboard. Kayak and SUP Amsterdam (run by Dutch kayak champion Rick Daman) organises paddle-boarding trips from its base next to the Berlagebrug (bridge) and close to the Amstel train station. After the trip, you can shower in its changing rooms then watch the world go by from the terrace bar by the river (kanoensupamsterdam.nl).

Richard Hammond's book The Green Traveller: Conscious Adventure that Doesn't Cost the Earth *is out now on Pavilion, priced £15.49.*

Recipe

Power Salads

Cooking on holiday needn't be a chore. Potato or couscous salads are simple to prepare, and make for super satisfying sides or mains.
By **Lindsey Bareham**

O N THE PIN BOARD behind my computer is a list of kitchen essentials to pack for a holiday let. I've been caught out too many times: no sharp knife, no bottle opener, no corkscrew and no matches. The list goes on, but those are the essentials. I bought a bright pink sharp knife (Kuhn Rikon, widely available) with a matching cover especially for holidays. It's so garish it won't get left behind.

Holiday cooking needs to be mindless and easy. Although it often revolves around the barbecue, it's the support system that needs a shopping list. I'm talking about the salads and stodge. I'm a big fan of couscous. Once you get the hang of preparing it, it's such a versatile, easy ingredient. To begin with I thought it adventurous to add toasted pine kernels or almonds to the hydrated couscous, bumping up the flavour with stock rather than water and colouring it with saffron. These days I make couscous salads all year round, varying what goes in depending on what's in season and

what needs eating up. Adding cooked peas and green beans with masses of herbs, particularly flat leaf parsley and mint, works well.

My other standbys for holiday cooking are potato salad and beetroot salad, which are very adaptable and go with most things.

Lemon Couscous with Chard and Caramelised Onion
Couscous salads are a favourite feed-the-5,000 standby and I always make too much because they keep perfectly in the fridge for a few days. They're a useful base for quick suppers and easy to liven up with extra herbs and add-ons like *boquerones* (Atlantic anchovies) or roasted Mediterranean vegetables. When I had an allotment, we grew a profusion of chard and it turned up in some surprising dishes like this salad. The couscous is flavoured with lemon and generously mixed with soft, silky, cooked chard, golden caramelised onion and toasted pine kernels. Hummus or tzatziki go well with it. For a

vegetarian feast, serve it with a few roasted tomato halves and griddled aubergine slices.

Serves 4–6
Prep: 20 min
Cook: 20 min
200g couscous
300ml boiling water
½ chicken stock cube
Generous pinch saffron stamens
1 large lemon
3tbsp olive oil
1 Spanish (very large) onion
30g pine kernels
200g chard or organic spinach

Fill and boil the kettle. Place the couscous in a mixing bowl. Dissolve the stock cube in 300ml boiling water. Stir in the saffron and leave to soften and bleed. Squeeze the lemon through a sieve into the stock. Stir again with 1tbsp olive oil and pour over the couscous. Stir thoroughly and cover the bowl with a tight stretch of clingfilm. Set aside for at least 15 min or until required. Halve the onion, trim the ends, remove the skin and slice very finely. Heat remaining oil in a spacious frying pan, stir in the onion and cook, stirring and adjusting the heat so it softens and turns golden without drying out or burning. Allow 15–20 min for this. When it looks almost ready, stir in the pine kernels and stir often as they get patched with gold. Turn off the heat. While the onions cook, fold the chard leaf along its stalk and slice down the stalk, cutting it from its leaf. Chop the stalks into 2cm lengths. Drop the stalks into a pan of salted boiling water from the kettle and after a few minutes add the leaves torn into 3 or 4 pieces depending on their size. Cook until tender then drain thoroughly. Slide the tines of a fork across the couscous, working down and continuing to separate the grains. Fork the chard loosely through the couscous. Add the onions and mix again. Pile onto a large shallow dish. A shower of pomegranate seeds goes well with this.

Turkish Beetroot Salad

Beetroot ticks so many boxes if it's treated right. I love it foil-wrapped and roasted with thyme and garlic, served with a squeeze of lemon and splash of my best olive oil (at the moment peppery extra virgin Federico Giuntini 2020 from the River Café). This recipe is a variation on that theme using boiled beets topped with sheep's yoghurt whipped with crushed garlic, lemon juice and olive oil. A satisfying salad, it goes with anything from hummus with tomato salad and crusty bread, to grilled mackerel, roast chicken or lamb kebabs.

Serves 2–4
Prep: 20 min
Cook: 20 min
500g boiled beetroot

1 lemon
1 garlic clove
250g thick, creamy yoghurt such as
Woodlands sheep milk yoghurt
1 tbsp olive oil
25g coriander

Cut the beets into bite-size chunks, place in a mixing bowl and squeeze lemon juice over the top. Season with salt and pepper, and toss. Pile into a shallow bowl. Crack the garlic, flake away the skin, finely chop and crush with a pinch of salt into a juicy paste. Add the garlic to the yoghurt in a second mixing bowl. Beat 1 tbsp olive oil into the yoghurt with a good squeeze of lemon. Spoon the yoghurt over the beets. Chop the coriander and scatter over the top. The lemony beetroot juices will bleed into the yoghurt. It's a very pretty, appealing dish.

Smoked Mackerel and Lemon Potato Salad

Many years ago, not long after Rick Stein opened in Padstow in 1975, The Seafood Restaurant started winning awards. In those days I was a restaurant critic and went to Newquay to interview Rick over lunch. What I particularly remember about the visit is the potatoes. I left clutching a bag of Cornish Earlies, and I'm very happy to say they're now widely available outside Cornwall. They're possibly my favourite new potatoes and unique in that they're harvested while the leaves are still green above the ground. Their flavour is intense, the skin soft and fluffy and the texture creamy and akin to waxy varieties like Jersey Royals and Belle de Fontenay. The rich flavour really adds to this salad but other new potatoes will be good. Peppery rocket instead of flat leaf parsley works well too.

Serves 2
Prep: 20 min
Cook: 15 min
350g small new potatoes
1 large or 2 small smoked
    mackerel fillets
Handful flat leaf parsley leaves
For the dressing:
1 tbsp mayonnaise
1 tbsp lemon juice
1 tbsp olive oil
2 tbsp creamed horseradish

Scrape, rinse and boil the potatoes in salted water. Drain and leave to cool. To make the dressing, spoon the mayo into a mixing bowl, beat in the lemon juice followed by the olive oil and the creamed horseradish. Stir the warm potatoes into the dressing. Flake the fish over the top in bite-size pieces taking care to remove any stray bones. Season lavishly with black pepper and use a spatula to mix the salad, turning rather than stirring. Chop the parsley and add it to the salad. Serve. 🐚

THE WORLD TODAY

CHATHAM HOUSE'S INTERNATIONAL AFFAIRS MAGAZINE
BRINGING RESEARCH TO LIFE SINCE 1945

SIX EDITIONS A YEAR | EXCLUSIVE ONLINE CONTENT INCLUDING
A SEARCHABLE ARCHIVE OF THE PAST 20 YEARS | WEEKLY INSIGHTS
INTO WORLD AFFAIRS | SUBSCRIPTIONS FROM £33

To subscribe go to www.theworldtoday.org. For any enquiries relating to marketing and
subscriptions, please contact Roxana Raileanu by email: RRaileanu@chathamhouse.org

MERRIMENT

Beer

Beyond the Pale

West Coast IPA or New England?
That's the question on **Oli Meade's** *lips*

I T'S A LITTLE after office hours and I'm in a queue at, of all places, a bar. "What can I get you?" asks the bartender as I make it to the front. He's wearing a baseball cap and wire-rimmed glasses, and he dons the obligatory modern-beer-moustache. He's smiling, enthusiastic and immediately likeable.

"I'll have a half of that Burnt Mill West Coast IPA please."

"This one?" He gestures to the only West Coast IPA pouring from the bar's ten taps. "You could definitely try this. But if you're after

an IPA, I'd go with this." He gestures again. "For my money, this is the best IPA we're pouring right now."

I glance in the direction of what he's suggesting. It is an IPA. But it's a New England IPA, as opposed to the West Coast IPA I was after, and I hesitate.

Should my fellow bartender really be suggesting I try a different beer?

Way Out West
Fairly regularly, curious patrons that drop into one of the Craft Metropolis taprooms down in south London ask me about the

Don't be afraid to ask: any question about beer is a good question

differences between West Coast and New England IPAs. Their enquiries are perfectly valid. They're about beer, after all, and any question about beer is a good one. Plus, the IPA is a pretty niche beer style in itself. So can its various sub-styles really be that different?

The surprising answer is yes: West Coast IPAs and New England IPAs are now so dissimilar it's probably time we started to think about a less confusing naming convention.

The West Coast IPA came along first, and was probably the beer style initially responsible for craft beer's worldwide explosion. The history books suggest the style was born over on the USA's West Coast, back when experimental homebrewers began adding unprecedented hop volumes to their brews in search of ever greater depths of flavour. Compared to the New England IPA

– or NEIPA, as it's become known – the West Coast IPA (WCIPA) was early stage experimentation. West Coast IPAs then and now were and remain relatively bitter (thanks to the hops), and any sweet notes derived from the style's malted barley are deliberately downplayed. In West Coast IPAs, the hops shine, which results in uninitiated drinkers invariably scrunching their faces post sip before describing WCIPAs as "too hoppy". What such drinkers usually mean is the WCIPA's distinct bitterness is unexpected. And it's unexpected because, these days, the beer drinkers' drink of choice is invariably the NEIPA.

A New England
New England IPAs are sometimes known as East Coast IPAs – which pinpoints their birthplace as that of the US East Coast. Whether deliberately or otherwise, the NEIPA is often positioned as a reaction to the WCIPA – the two styles contrast in looks, in aroma and in taste.

West Coast IPAs – which usually sit on a backbone of malted barley – are typically amber in colour and transparent in nature. New England IPAs? Their colour profiles vary, but they often lean towards yellow. Undeniably more striking is the fact that they're opaque (or "hazy"), which is the result of the NEIPA's malt profile. Typically, brewers use a combination of barley, wheat and/

or oats in their NEIPAs' malt bills, which make NEIPAs soft and creamy – a characteristic that's proving increasingly popular.

You can expect both West Coast and New England IPAs to carry fruity aromas… but the overlap is rarely sizeable. From a West Coast IPA you might detect some citrus, but it'll invariably be cloaked in powerful aromas of some form of foliage – pine is the go-to and fresh cut grass is another favourite. Increasingly, notes of "dank" cannabis waft from the WCIPA's glass.

By contrast, any New England IPA that doesn't smell like a tropical fruit punch should be treated with suspicion. In a New England IPA, I'm looking for stuff like mango, passionfruit, papaya and cantaloupe melon, and maybe even a sprinkle of coconut (depending on the hops on showcase). And while it's possible for a beer's aromas to differ from its flavours, in my experience, such discrepancies are rare.

We've already touched on the differences in flavour but to spell it out: West Coast IPAs are usually bright, piney and resinous, possibly sweaty, sometimes fruity and, of course, their biting bitterness lingers. By contrast, New England IPAs tend to be so laden with fruit they're described as "juicy". NEIPAs are usually tropical and most likely to be a little sweet, with very little bitterness. Oats and wheat, when used, give NEIPAs a creamy quality.

The two styles are both outstanding, and just as I love stouts, saisons, lambics, goses, lagers, pales and porters, I adore both WCIPAs and NEIPAs in turn.

Still, they're not the same thing, and sometimes you know precisely what you want.

Doing It By Halves

I think about all the above back at the bar, where the (increasingly delightful) bartender is gesturing towards his favoured NEIPA, still with a big grin on his face, hoping to convince me to go with his suggestion.

"You know what?" I say. "Give me a half of the West Coast and a half of the New England."

He's even more delighted than he might otherwise have been, and as I take the two halves back to a table, so am I.

Craft beer. It's all about experimentation but is West Coast the best coast? Only you can decide.

Four to Try

Verdant Brewing Co – Even Sharks Need Water NEIPA

Cornwall's Verdant is seen as one of the UK's best craft breweries, and Even Sharks Need Water is one of the brewery's regular gems. Fruity, juicy and tropical; thick, creamy and soft. A great example of a solid New England IPA.

Pressure Drop Brewery – Behind Door Number 3 NEDIPA

Pressure Drop are no strangers to supplying drinkers with juice, and in Behind Door Number 3 they amp up the NEIPA to Double IPA territory. Soft, fruity, tropical and strong. This isn't the thickest beer, but it packs a punch.

Verdant Brewing Co – Remembering Things I Didn't Do WCIPA

The periodically rebrewed Remembering Things I Didn't Do shows what Verdant can do when armed with West Coast hops. This is citrusy and bright, clean and bitter. Dank notes complete the West Coast ensemble.

Burnt Mill Brewery – Get The Onyx WCIPA

Underrated all-rounders Burnt Mill flex their West Coast might with this clean and crisp WCIPA. Expect piney bitterness with hints of passionfruit. Warning: this thing reeks of weed. 🐌

Oli Meade owns and runs Craft Metropolis, an independent craft beer taproom and shop based in London. You can visit Craft Metropolis Brixton and Craft Metropolis Penge, or get beer recommendations from Oli at craftmetropolis.co.uk.

Eating Out
La Dolce Villa

Victoria Hull *visits a truly Tuscan restaurant on Chiswick High Road*

VILLA DI GEGGIANO in Chiswick, west London, is in a large plain white house with green shutters set behind high black railings and a vine-covered terrace. It's named after a palatial villa in Tuscany owned by the aristocratic Bianchi Bandinelli family, who now sell their wine to the restaurant, and help run it.

The building has a chequered history. It was once a working men's club with a dance floor "and a fight a week" according to locals, then a pizzeria. After that Marco Pierre White ran it but his marriage was breaking down, the vibes were bad and the place was failing.

Enter Polish entrepreneur Ilona Pacia and her husband. In 2014 they took over the building, with money made from their successful cleaning facilities company, and, working in partnership with the Bianchi

Vine and dine: Sangiovese plants grow overhead in the shady terrace

Bandinellis, renamed the restaurant Villa Di Geggiano. Ilona says she didn't like anything in the restaurant except the black and white tiled floor that matched Marco's enthusiasm for black and white checked bandanas, Vans trainers and tabards.

Ilona's own choice of decoration reflects the elegance of Villa di Geggiano's namesake in Tuscany. But she's also put her mark on it. She's packed the walls with art and brought in resident artists and curators from a previous business running an art gallery. She's determined to make Villa di Geggiano a welcoming home for the arts and is thrilled when stars from the next-door recording studios Metropolis come to dine. "We've had Snoop Dogg here, Will.i.am,

Shaggy and Pharrell Williams. Director Sir Trevor Nunn and explorer Bruce Parry are regulars."

The original Tuscan Villa di Geggiano and its vineyards have been owned for five centuries by the Bianchi Bandinelli family and are now run by brothers Andrea and Alessandro. Their grandfather Ranuccio Bianchi Bandinelli was a renowned archaeologist and art historian who was employed by Mussolini to show Hitler around Rome. (Ranuccio said Hitler was "hungry for knowledge" and Mussolini was "an ignorant pig".)

After the war Ranuccio, disgusted by fascism, turned Marxist. He worked for the government as director of its Fine Arts and Antiquities department. Fittingly, he turned his wine-growing estates into communes and gave 25 out of 26 of them to his workers, keeping only Villa Geggiano for himself.

The family seems still imbued with communist principles, to the occasional frustration of the entrepreneurial Ilona: when she started the restaurant's cigar room, where you can smoke Tuscan cigars at the end of dinner, the brothers wanted to give the cigars away for free. This was an idea that Ilona quickly quashed.

A further glittery connection comes in the form of Tuscany-dwelling Sting and his wife Trudie. They make wine on their estate, which is next door to the original Villa di Geggiano, and collaborate with Ilona on her wine list. Some are named after Sting's songs, like "Roxanne" and "Message in a Bottle". "People can snipe," says Ilona, "but Trudie and Sting can afford the very best expertise so they can make the very best wine."

When you arrive at the gates of the restaurant you get a warm welcome. Grandly caped, smiling doormen usher you across the terrace and Lukasz the manager is ready at the door to make you feel expected and special. We are settled quickly onto sofas in the cocktail lounge. The walls are packed tight with paintings including Bianchi Bandinelli family portraits and photographs. A glass of softly

The Gallery private dining room with artworks chosen by Ilona

The menu is classic Tuscan

bubbling pink Prosecco surprises us by its deliciousness and by not giving us instant headaches – a good sign of having no sulphites.

The menu is classic Tuscan. Antipasti of focaccia, chunky green olives, crispy seeded bread sticks. We try *primi* of pork rib ravioli, pappardelle with wild boar, classic black spaghetti and Cacio e Pepe, that simple spaghetti dish with just Parmesan and pepper. For *secondi* a gorgonzola risotto is perfect, grilled squid stuffed with mussels a little challenging, and a duck fillet tender, pink and salty. We finish with crema cotta with caramelised nuts and a delicious tiramisu laden

Dining room

with cocoa. I'd forgotten what classy food tasted like. The tables are double layered with white linen, the glasses crafted with Villa di Gegggiano crests, and the waiters caring and personal.

Villa di Geggiano has a classic Italian homely feel for a special occasion dinner. But you can also have a very reasonable lunch under the loggia, shaded by Sangiovese vines, sipping Sangiovese grape wine, and easily imagine yourself in a Tuscan wine estate. You might just notice that the green shutters on the white house are actually trompe l'œil. Get yourself onto the newsletter and pop in for an arts event. The *Idler* may well be there.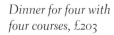

*Dinner for four with
four courses, £203*

Lunch menu two courses, £25

Villa di Geggiano
66–68 Chiswick High Road,
London W4 1SY
villadigeggiano.co.uk
020 3384 9442

Ukulele
The Tall Guy

Cameron Murray *pays tribute to an outsider player/singer whose distinctive style saw him shoot to fame in the sixties, performing for the Beatles and the Stones*

I RECENTLY PRESENTED a workshop on the history of the ukulele and when I mentioned Tiny Tim, a groan of disapproval arose from the audience. It was exactly the response I expected. Perhaps no other well-known musician has been so badly maligned.

Now, before you rip out this page in a rage, please allow me to explain…

While he was never the greatest player in the world, Tiny Tim is an important part of the story of the uke. From the late 1960s to the mid-1990s, his name was synonymous with the instrument, much in the way George Formby had been in the 1940s and Jake Shimabukuro is now. At a time when the ukulele was taking a back seat to guitar-driven pop and electronica, Tiny was proudly flying the four-string flag.

Born Herbert Khaury in New York City on 12 April, 1932, he was fascinated with music from an early age. In fact, Herbie's first memory was of a song, Henry Burr's 1919 hit "Beautiful Ohio".

Herbie absorbed popular tunes from the 1890s to the 1930s like a sponge and had an incredible memory for lyrics – so much so that it's estimated he knew 10,000 songs by heart. With a clear vision for his future, he dropped out of high school in classic idler fashion and turned his attention to becoming a star.

In the 1950s, American media personality Arthur Godfrey championed the ukulele. He'd learnt to play while serving in the navy and would often sing and strum on his daily radio programme and two weekly TV shows. He even hosted televised uke lessons. When Godfrey endorsed Mario Maccaferri's brand-new plastic ukulele, Herbie immediately bought one, along with nine million other people. He needed an instrument to accompany his unique voice and the uke was relatively easy to learn and portable. It didn't even need a case – an old shopping bag would do.

After 12 years of constant struggle and a few name changes, Tiny Tim (he was actually 6ft 1in) started to make an impact in New York's thriving Greenwich Village music scene of the early sixties. He was befriended by Bob Dylan and soon attracted of a cult following.

Towards the end of the decade, everything was going right for Tiny. In 1968, he released *God Bless Tiny Tim*, the album that included his biggest hit, "Tip-Toe Thru' the Tulips with Me", and he played a once-in-a-lifetime show at London's Royal Albert Hall, with both the Beatles and the Rolling Stones in attendance.

On 17 December, 1969, Tiny married Victoria Budinger, *aka* Miss Vicki, live on *The Tonight Show Starring Johnny Carson* in front of 40 million viewers, cementing his fame.

Over the next couple of decades Tiny's celebrity waned and he became little more than a grotesque caricature in many people's eyes. But when the ukulele made a comeback in the early 1990s, so did he.

Tiny began appearing at uke festivals and clearly loved the adulation, but sadly his health was on the decline. At the Ukulele Hall of Fame Museum's Ukulele Expo '96 in Massachusetts, he had a minor heart attack and collapsed on stage. On 30 November, 1996,

during a gig at The Woman's Club of Minneapolis and still holding his beloved Martin soprano uke, he suffered a massive heart attack and was pronounced dead shortly afterwards.

"He died singing "Tip-Toe Thru' the Tulips", the last thing he heard was applause, and the last person he saw was me," said his third wife Sue Gardner. "It was just like Tiny to die like that. He was a born showman."

No matter what you think of his music or idiosyncrasies, Tiny kept the ukulele in the public consciousness when the odds were stacked against it. What he achieved was a revolutionary act worthy of any punk rocker. He was absolutely determined to do what he loved and make it a success, no matter how difficult it was or what anybody thought of him. He was a true artist.

God bless Tiny Tim. 🐌

Spirits

The Gunpowder Tot

The days of sailors' tot rations may have gone, but Royal Navy rum lives on in a Caribbean brand that uses the Admiralty's own blend – and it's not for the faint-hearted, says **Joseph Piercy**

RUM HAS HISTORICALLY had a strong association with seafaring, be it through the swash-buckling romance of pirates and buccaneers, the nefarious activities of smugglers and rum-runners, or the more sombre and cynical military machinations of colonialism.

In particular, its association with the Royal Navy is steeped in eccentric ritual and colourful colloquialisms. The tradition of providing rum as part of the navy's basic daily rations dates back to the mid-17th century and Britain's capture of Jamaica from the Spanish in 1655. The necessity of maintaining a military presence in the Caribbean to protect British imperial interests entailed seamen spending lengthy periods at sea and enduring long and often hazardous voyages. Stocks of drinking water and beer would become contaminated over time and virtually undrinkable, hence rum provided an easily available, cheap and efficient solution.

The practice of providing a ship's crew with alcohol rations was also seen as beneficial in terms of maintaining morale, and there was some evidence the ration was increased prior to military engagements to embolden the men. The ledger *In Relation to His Majesty's Services at Sea* of 1731 records the daily ration as half a pint of rum or brandy, plus a gallon of beer. That's eight pints of beer and ten double shots of spirits. Granted, the beer was probably fairly low in alcohol compared with most modern beers, but nonetheless, rampant drunkenness and alcoholism were certainly problems on naval ships.

Admiral Edward Vernon was the man responsible for ritualising the delivery of the daily rum ration. Mindful of the welfare of the men under his command, on 21 August 1740, Vernon issued Captain's Order No. 349, which decreed that the rum ration should be diluted with "one quart water" (two pints) and dispensed in two equal portions twice daily (at noon and the end of the working day). Vernon's reasoning was that by spreading out the distribution of the rum and diluting the alcohol, the men under his command wouldn't be able to get quite so pissed, quite so quickly.

The delivery of the ration was preceded by a short bugle blast, followed by the cry of "Up spirits!" by the ship's purser. This was the ceremonial signal for the chief petty officer to retrieve the keys to the Spirit Room, where the barrels of rum were kept, closely guarded (for obvious reasons). The rum rations were carefully measured into separate kegs and mixed with the water to the required ratio under the watchful supervision of the purser, the ship's cooper and a group of Royal Marines.

Once the requisite amount of rum had been measured out, this varied from day to day, as seaman under charges for drunken misdemeanours were issued temporary bans and forced to drink some unspeakable substitute as punishment), the keg was carried under armed procession to the ship's deck to be dispensed to the officers and ratings. The rum ration became known as "grog" in naval circles, in honour of Admiral Vernon, who famously always sported a tatty grogram greatcoat when on deck duty, leading to his nickname of Old Grog.

By the latter half of 19th century attitudes to drinking in Britain had markedly cooled, led by the rise of the temperance movements. The British navy had made several attempts to review the dispensing of the rum ration, even setting up a "Grog Committee" to research and report on alcoholism on naval ships. However, the navy could never quite bring themselves to abolish it completely, instead gradually reducing the size of the ration and diluting it further. Remarkably, the rum ration survived until 1970, when its abolition was debated in the House of Commons. Giving evidence to the House, Chief of Naval Staff, Admiral Somerfield Teagle acknowledged the historical tradition and ceremony of "the tot" but argued that the dispensing of rations of strong alcohol in "a high technology service which places great emphasis on individual responsibility" was "simply not appropriate". The final bugle blast and cry of "Up spirits!" on British naval ships took place on 31 July 1970, a day recorded in naval folklore as "Black Tot Day".

Almost a decade after the last barrel of Royal Navy rum was emptied, Charles Tobias, an entrepreneur based in the British Virgin Islands, approached the navy for the rights to produce the rum blend as a commercial enterprise. Tobias had supposedly researched the blending notes for the original navy rums and registered his brand as Pusser's, in honour of a ship's purser who was responsible for administering the tot. As part of the deal, Tobias cannily offered to donate a percentage of sales to naval related charities. For the perennially cash strapped Royal Navy (or so they would have us believe), the offer was too good to refuse.

Pusser's signature rum is their Gunpowder Strength 54.5% Navy Rum. The name derives from the old practice, dating back to 17th century, of testing "the proof" of rum by mixing a small amount with a little gunpowder and heating the mixture over a flame. The colour and intensity at which the rum and gunpowder mixture burned determined the "proof" (strength) of the quality of the rum. Originally, overproof was rum containing 57.5%ABV (alcohol by volume) as determined by the gunpowder test, however, the navy, being sticklers for uniformity, conducted extensive tests on hundreds of barrels of the navy tot and downgraded the overproof level to 54.5%. The question of what constitutes overproof and what constitutes "navy strength" is a pedant's delight so in short. Any rum over 50% ABV is generally considered overproof.

As may be expected from a very strong spirit, Pusser's Gunpowder Strength benefits from adding a little cold water and one piece of ice – drinking it warm and neat is not for the faint-hearted. How authentic Pusser's is in terms of the rum used as grog is hard to determine as what little remains of the original Royal Navy rum stocks are in the hands of wily collectors and sell for eye-watering prices at auctions. The blend Pusser's uses incorporates rums from several parts of the Caribbean but is produced in the British Virgin Islands, all of which sounds very much like a shrewd marketing scam, but I doubt the Royal Navy cares one tot while they're getting a cut of the profits. 🐚

SELF

Being Well

Are We All Mad?

Rachel Kelly *on the thorny subject of diagnosing mental illness*

A RE YOU SUFFERING from a mental health condition? Or are you just dealing with what Freud called "ordinary human unhappiness?" And how would you know the difference?

Welcome to the tricky world of diagnosing mood disorders – the universe of anxiety and depression, post-traumatic stress disorder, obsessive compulsive disorder and being "on the spectrum". Exactly how to decide if you're a sufferer or not is an area that's currently being debated by mental health professionals and patients like me: I suffered two severe depressive

episodes in my thirties, though I'm now recovered.

One argument runs roughly like this: the current diagnostic system is still largely based on a description of a series of symptoms reported by the patient. Unlike with physical illnesses, we have no blood test or brain scan that can positively identify if someone is suffering from depression or ADHD. And although mental health problems are often compared to physical ones – "It's no different to breaking a leg" – actually, that may not be true when it comes to the complexities of diagnosis.

What's more, as the historian and professor of sociology and science studies at the University of California, Andrew Scull, points out in his new book, *Desperate Remedies: Psychiatry and the Mysteries of Mental Illness*, it can be possible for patients diagnosed with the same condition to share no symptoms whatsoever.

Partly because of the uncertainties around diagnosis, there has been an explosion in the number of people who doctors have identified as suffering from mood disorders. There are now so many possible mental health conditions that the *Diagnostic and Statistical Manual of Mental Disorders* – the definitive publication on this subject – now runs to 500 pages. The first edition in 1952 was just 100 pages. The number of people in the UK taking antidepressants has been rising steadily since their introduction, and is now at around 7.6 million people.

Practically every family I know has someone with a diagnosis of a mental health or psychological condition. And it's almost par for the course for famous people. Indeed, the TV personality and aristocratic cook Gizzi Erskine, 42, who has spoken openly about struggling with anxiety, attention deficit hyperactivity disorder and depression, says so many people claim to suffer from ADHD that they're clogging up NHS waiting lists, preventing genuinely sick people from receiving treatment. "I'm almost certain that people now want the diagnosis because it seems cool and not because they're genuinely ADHD," she says.

Meanwhile Dame Joanna Lumley has said the "mental health thing" is being "overplayed" at the moment, because anybody who's even remotely sad says they've got mental problems, when what they're really suffering from is simply "what's called being human".

So this first argument might be summarised as "we have pathologised normal human behaviour using possibly questionable diagnostic tools, and far too many people have been wrongly diagnosed with a mental health condition". For those who subscribe to this view, even the phrase "mental illness" is suspect. They prefer to talk about mental health problems rather than saying someone is suffering from an "illness".

Yet others, including most psychiatrists, take a different view: that diagnostic tools *are* reliable. Professor Carmine Pariante, a psychiatrist at King's College London, is one such doctor. "We have very reliable ways to ask the key questions to understand what is the mental disorder that someone might be suffering from," he says. "A good interview from a psychiatrist or a psychologist is as accurate as any interview, blood test or X-ray scan from a cardiologist or a cancer specialist."

Prof Pariante also challenges Scull's point that patients diagnosed with the same condition might not share any conditions. "Again, this is a myth," he says. "Yes, two people with a diagnosis of depression may have different profiles of secondary symptoms – for example, one person might want to eat or sleep less than usual, and another might want to eat or sleep more – but they will all have the same core symptoms of persistent sadness and decreased day-to-day abilities to work and socialise."

He continues: "If they're not sad, by definition they're not depressed. The same is true for anxiety, or psychosis, or ADHD: there are core symptoms that are essential for the diagnosis and that are present in all people with that mental disorder."

Those who take this view believe that many people who are suffering from mental health conditions are not being diagnosed. Many don't want to report their mental distress because stigma still lingers, they say. There is fear of loss of employment.

So what is the truth? Is it somewhere between these views? Is there any consensus? In fact there is some common ground. One area of consensus is that we need to distinguish between mild and more serious conditions, as indeed

psychiatrists routinely do when they make their diagnoses. Dr Jamie Arkell, a psychiatrist at the Nightingale Hospital, says that the most important factor in diagnosing any psychiatric disorder is "the level of disability".

Let's get personal. Severe depression is the most terrifying thing that has ever happened to me. I have never, ever felt so unwell. I was suicidal – not because I didn't enjoy a pleasant life, but because I couldn't bear the physical pain any longer.

At the time, I was relieved to be diagnosed with severe depressive disorder, via a list of symptoms, by a psychiatrist, to whom I entrusted my life. I was treated with medication and was lucky not to stay on antidepressants for more than a few years. Did I have a diagnosable illness? Given the severity and physicality of my symptoms, I am tempted to say, yes I did. But I will never know for sure.

A second point of agreement is that diagnosis should consider a patient's circumstances and social situation – what doctors call a "psychosocial assessment". Luckily, this is now common practice among psychiatrists. In addition, psychologists, therapists, and counsellors are also able to make a psychosocial assessment. Mental suffering is not just due to physical causes or symptoms, but is embedded in our upbringing and our current social and personal circumstances. Such assessments are more likely to lead to a realistic picture of whether someone really has a mental health problem or is just dealing with life's everyday ups and downs.

A final point of agreement is on the need for more support for those who are suffering. While arguments around diagnosis will continue, the suffering of those in mental distress is very, very real, as I know from experience. I was able to get support, which many others today can't. We need to keep looking out for those with severe problems.

It's true that the system is being clogged with the worried well: I agree with Dame Joanna's view that we need to "get a grip" because mental health services are currently overrun, waiting lists are dire, and those who are really in need of treatment can't access help.

The mental health charity Mind estimates that only one in eight adults with mental health problems are currently getting any treatment. Those with severe problems aren't getting enough support. That's a scandal, and one point on which we can all agree.

" I'm afraid we cannot continue all the while Mr Bojangles keeps calling me a nosey twat "

The Idle Investor
Putting it Behind Bars

Should idlers invest in gold or bitcoin?
By Dominic Frisby

THE OLDEST EVIDENCE of humans using metal are fragments of gold found in Spanish caves inhabited by Paleolithic people, dating back perhaps 40,000 years. The first record of humans using copper came tens of thousands of years later. Lead, tin and iron first came into use even later.

Paleolithic man decorated himself with gold, along with shells and beads, to denote his great status. "Look at me," he was saying. "I have access to this shiny, captivating metal." He used it as a gift, or as a reward – "Well done for hunting down that beast." Or he used it to barter. In other words, gold was primitive money.

Its function hasn't changed. We still use it to store wealth, and to display it. We also give it in gifts, and occasionally use it in trade.

The problem gold has in today's fast-moving world, where almost all the value is now digital, is that it's a physical asset. The result of asteroid strikes and supernovae collisions, it's probably the oldest substance on earth. It's also the most durable. You can smash it into a film one atom thick, but you can't destroy it (though you can dissolve it in *aqua regia*). As a result, pretty much all the gold that has ever been mined still exists in the world today.

But gold is still non-digital. It might be sexy to look at, but in terms of its price action, it's anything but. Despite the gazillions of pounds, dollars and euros that have been printed, it's still trading below where it was ten years ago.

And yet both Russia and China have been accumulating tonnes of the stuff. China is the world's biggest producer. It doesn't export a single gram. It's also the world's largest importer. In all likelihood it has ten times more gold than it admits to. It also has designs on global currency status and, having seen how the US froze Russia's 400 billion plus dollars and told them it would never get them back, China's going to need alternatives for its trillion plus US dollar holdings if it doesn't want to be the US's puppy. You can bet Russia feels the same.

Stated inflation is seven per cent. Actual inflation as felt by citizens is much higher. Have you tried to buy a house lately? The purchasing power of the pound and the dollar are being gradually and constantly eroded. Gold's time is going to come again. Keep some savings outside the system is my advice, where they can't get at them.

Enter bitcoin, the newest money system in the world, anything but physical. With bitcoin you can send fractions of a penny or billions of dollars anywhere in the world instantaneously and there's nothing the US, Russian, British or Chinese government can do about it (as long as you've got an internet connection). It's a new system of borderless, non-government money for the borderless medium that is the internet.

When every CEO of every company in the world, particularly Nasdaq companies, sees their company treasures being eroded at around ten per cent a year by inflation, they have a fiduciary duty to shareholders to start using alternate savings vehicles. That's where bitcoin comes in. More and more CEOs, especially of tech companies, will follow Michael Saylor and Elon Musk's lead and convert their treasuries to bitcoin, which is a considerably better store of value and a considerably more convenient system of money (you don't need to get the bank's permission to use it). Its price is up 10 times in the last two years, 100 times in the last five, 10,000 times in the last ten. The latest correction is a mere blip in an upward trajectory on this relentless march forward for this most anarchist, subversive and anti-authoritarian of technologies.

So, dear idlers, follow China's lead, follow Elon Musk's lead, own both, then do nothing. HODL is the rallying cry of bitcoiners. A typo. It means hold and do nothing. An idler's rallying call if ever there was one. Why should your savings or salary, the product of your sweat and labour, become a tool for some government you don't like and whose policies you don't agree with? Channel your inner anarchist and stick it to the man.

And if you want to learn more about investing in either gold or bitcoin, my Substack is the place.

Check out Dominic's Substack at frisby.substack.com – *Make Money and Stick It to the Man.*

Problems
Virginia Ironside

Our agony aunt sorts you out

Dad Vice

My husband refers to looking after our children as "babysitting". He tells his friends, forlornly, that he can't come and play five-a-side football because he has to "be on dad duty". He's actually brilliant with the kids, but his childishness really pisses me off. Should I live and let live?

Sarah, Surrey

I FIND IT VERY odd that you refer to his remarks as evidence of "childishness". I can't help wondering, hoping that I don't sound too much like a therapist, if your irritation isn't about something more than these totally harmless remarks. Do you feel that he is too childish sometimes – and do you find his childishness annoying? A lot of successful partners find that their roles are constantly changing – sometimes one partner feels weak and dependent on the other; other times it's the reverse. Then other days they find they have a good relationship as equals. However responsible and strong we may appear, all of us can become fragile beings, often with sudden lapses into babyish and child-like states. Most of us not only understand these moods, but find them rather touching and like to find vulnerability in our partners – not always, but from time to time. The language he's using may be due to lack of confidence, or a wishing not to be seen as some macho father figure all the time.

Don't Whistle While You Work

A colleague in my office has the horrible habit of whistling while he works. Yes, it might seem charming and I'm glad he enjoys his job, but it is infuriating. I don't want to come across as a killjoy, but he's driving me to distraction. How do I confront him?

Helen, north London

L IKE YOU I'D be driven nuts by permanent whistling – just as much as I find next door's radio intolerable. You could confront him, though I imagine it wouldn't be a very pleasant conversation for either of you. You could try to rise above it and zone it out – no doubt some practised meditator could help you. Or you could think of his whistling as a sign of a deep fear of silence, and try to feel more charitable about it, as if it were a tic that he couldn't help – which I suspect it is. Ask around the office to see if anyone else minds it as much as you do – it would help to find an ally. Failing all this, you could try earplugs.

Mama Don't Preach

My mother has become incredibly moralistic in her older age. She phones me up just to tell me off for not giving to charity (I do), staying out late (I don't) and for anything else she can come up with. I feel like a naughty teenager again, but I'm almost 40. Help!
Abbey, Brighton

I SUSPECT THAT, like a lot of older, lonely people, your mother feels she's losing her power over you, her child – which, of course, she is. You can either have a row about it, which will upset both of you, or you could try to find some area of your life in which she could, indeed, be a help. If you could make her feel needed and useful, and be grateful for her contribution, I think this criticism would stop. Or at least lessen.

Pay Pals

A close friend of mine and her partner run a very expensive restaurant. Business for them is thriving, whereas I live like a church mouse. I visited said restaurant (at their invitation) last week and at the end of the meal was presented with a huge bill. I refused to pay. Am I an awful person?
Paul, Essex

IT DEPENDS HOW you refused. If you were rude and shouty then that wasn't a good call. But you could have expressed surprise when faced with the bill and said to the waiting person that you were certain this was on the house. You'd been asked specially by the owner, you could say, and understood it was a gift. Had you known you had to pay you wouldn't have come – not because you didn't want to but because you simply couldn't afford it. You should then have asked them to sort out the "misunderstanding" (which it might have been) with your friends, assuring them that had you got the wrong end of the stick you would be happy to pay a part of the bill later. Obviously if you get no joy then you'll have to ring your friends to sort it out – knowing that you may risk the friendship if there was indeed a huge misunderstanding. 🐚

Readers' Letters

Write to us at mail@idler.co.uk or Readers' Letters,
Idler, Great Western Studios, 65 Alfred Road, London W2 5EU.
Please include a mailing address with your letter.
Star letter wins a signed copy of An Idler's Manual by Tom Hodgkinson

★★★ Star Letter ★★★

Floating Loafer

Sir: Nearly 50 years ago, a certain writer praised baths. "Turning the tap with one's toes", he wrote, "is the mark of the true bather, and few sensations are more pleasurable than, when one's bath has become a little tepid, feeling the new hot water slowly lap up one's body and once again one is wrapped in it." The writer in question, who happened to be my father, went on to explain that he did not encounter the shower until he first visited America in the 1960s. He reckoned Americans' incessant showering had a lot to do with their being "always on the go, never able to take things quietly", leading them to seek compensation through self-actualisation therapies and the like. "Only a nation that showers instead of taking baths would have to pay money to be taught how to meditate and relax." Showers, like so many other American cultural preferences, are now fully established in Britain, where we are encouraged to take them because, we are told, they use less water than baths. This is poppycock, since it depends entirely upon how long one showers for, and how often. If it takes seven minutes to run a bath, then seven minutes of running a shower at the same pressure will use the same volume of water. The difference is that the shower only lasts seven minutes, while you get at least half an hour of immersion from the bath, and even longer if you apply your foot to the hot tap for an extra minute or two. A bath, I maintain, refreshes both body and mind more profoundly and more lastingly, whereas a shower is a quick fix. I know people who have a dozen showers for every bath I take. For those of us with workaholic tendencies, taking a bath offers the perfect excuse for relaxing, lolling weightlessly, daydreaming, pondering and planning, musing and snoozing, while the water does the work of washing away bodily impurities. With a bit of practice it is possible to read in the bath, and for this purpose I constructed a book-rest on one of those racks that straddle the bath to hold your soap, sponge and rubber duck. Unfortunately, no sooner had I perfected the device than my eyesight started to go, I needed glasses, and glasses mist up in the bath.

Simon Fairlie, Dorset

Classic Conundrum

Sir: I know you avoid politics, but I've been wondering what an anti-government protest in Latin would look like, on the grounds that "it's the only language these people understand". Can't be sure whether the conceit is amusing enough to warrant any scholarship, but if it were, it occurred to me your crack team of Mounts and Vernons might have fun with it, or spin off into talking about protest in the ancient world.

Paul Flowers

Not Bringing Back the Bacon

Sir: I would argue that "bacon" should be dropped from the Idler's "Freedom Manifesto" (which currently declares "Beer, Bread, Bacon."). Vegan or not (I'm a vegan), enjoying life certainly is less joyful if it's at the expense of

someone else's life (an art developed to perfection by neoliberal capitalists and other happy sociopaths whose joy on earth does not extend much farther than the confines of their own physical selves). So I woke up this morning here in the Hollywood Hills with a possible replacement that no idler could possibly object to: "Dream, Drink, Dine."

Stig Harder, California

Up in Smoke

Sir: Do you know these Idlerish lines from the poem "Hotel", by the French poet Guillaume Apollinaire?

My room's shaped like a cage
The sun
Puts his arm right through
  the window
But I, who wish to smoke and
  dream
use it to light my cigarette
I don't want to work,
  I want to smoke.
Gill, via email 🐌

153

Puzzle
Letters play

by **Alex Bellos**

THE FOLLOWING WORDS are all partially obscured. The first one, for example, is PUZZLE. What are the other words? They all describe leisure activities, and the alphabet used is:

ABCDEFGHIJKLMNOPQRSTUVWXYZ

PUZZLE   PICNIC

CLUEDO   TENNIS

KARATE   BOULES

HIKING   BRIDGE

Answers on page 160.
A new edition of The Language Lover's Puzzle Book
by Alex Bellos is out now, published by Guardian Faber.

155

NEW

Consider the Trees with Colin Tudge
3 hrs 15 mins across six videos

The world-renowned biologist gives six talks on what trees are, how they work, and why we need to give them more respect. Informative, scientific and awe-inspiring in equal measure, this course is essential for anyone interested in the natural world.

NEW

How To Write with John-Paul Flintoff
1 hr 50 mins across six videos

One of the best ways to become a writer is to sneak up on yourself by practicing, and suddenly find that you're writing. In this practical course with journalist and author John-Paul Flintoff, you'll quickly set aside worries about being "any good", and get on with finding your voice.

NEW

Dante's Divine Comedy in 100 Images with Dr Mark Vernon
4 hrs 27 mins across ten videos

Psychotherapist Dr Vernon is your guide through Dante's Divine Comedy. Join him for a journey of self-discovery, taking in hell, purgatory and heaven.

The Seasonal Festivals of Britain with Prof Ronald Hutton
1 hr 50 mins across four videos

Join Professor of Modern History Ronald Hutton for his spirited and illustrated journey through the seasonal festivals of Britain from May Day revelry to midsummer fires, Christmas feasts to harvest parties. Along the way, you'll learn about British folklore traditions, the real significance of the May Pole, why the Puritans banned Christmas, and the magical properties of St John's Wort.

Italian Literature with Henry Eliot

Author and literary podcaster Henry Eliot takes us through the greatest books of Italian literature. His entertaining talks survey the entire history of it, from Rome to the Renaissance, Romanticism to the Risorgimento, Modernism to Post-Modernism. This is your chance to make sure you know all the greatest Italian authors, including Virgil, Ovid, Dante, Boccaccio, Machiavelli, Manzoni, Svevo and Calvino.

 idler.co.uk/join

English Language

How to Write with John-Paul Flintoff
1 hr 50 mins across six videos

**How to Write a Poem
with Clare Pollard**
2 hrs 30 mins across seven videos

Punctuation with Harry Mount
43 mins across one video lesson

**Elocution with
Sir Timothy Ackroyd**
2 hrs 7 mins across four videos

Literature

**Dante's Divine Comedy in
100 Images with Mark Vernon**
4 hrs 27 mins across ten videos

**What Matters in Jane Austen
with Professor John Mullan**
1 hr 45 mins across four videos

**An Introduction to Medieval English
Literature with Henry Eliot**
2 hrs 22 mins across six videos

**The Life and Works of Charles
Dickens, Series One: Young
Celebrity, with Henry Eliot**
2 hrs 40 mins across six videos

**The Life and Works of Charles
Dickens, Series Two: Dark
Genius, with Henry Eliot**
2 hrs 50 mins across six videos

**The Life and Works of Charles
Dickens, Series Three: Social
Critic, with Henry Eliot**
2 hrs 55 mins across six videos

**An Introduction to Borges
with Henry Eliot**
2 hrs 40 mins across six videos

Philosophy

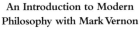

**How to be Idle with
Tom Hodgkinson**
2 hrs 40 mins across six videos

**An Introduction to Ancient
Philosophy with Mark Vernon**
4 hrs 35 mins across six videos

**An Introduction to Plato's
Dialogues with Mark Vernon
and Tom Hodgkinson**
2 hrs 48 mins across six videos

**An Introduction to Modern
Philosophy with Mark Vernon**
2 hours 30 mins across six videos

**A History of Christianity in Eleven
Short Chapters with Dr Mark Vernon**
3 hrs 51 mins across eleven videos

**Romantic Philosophy
with Mark Vernon**
1 hr 10 mins across three videos

**Eastern Philosophy and Alan
Watts with Tim Lott**
3 hrs 8 mins across six videos

**A Brief Introduction to Anarchism
with Tom Hodgkinson**
40 mins across three videos

**How to Build Your Own Utopia
with David Bramwell**
2 hrs across six videos

**Introduction to Psychotherapy
with Mark Vernon**
1 hr 55 mins across six videos

**The Idler Guide to Imagination
with Mark Vernon**
2 hrs 30 mins across three videos

 idler.co.uk/online-courses

JOIN THE IDLER
ACADEMY FOR £95

Music

An Introduction to Classical Music with Sandy Burnett
3 hrs 45 mins across seven videos

The Idler Guide to Jazz with Sandy Burnett
1 hr 50 mins across eight videos

The Idler Guide to British Folk with Will Hodgkinson
2 hrs 10 mins across six videos

How to Write a Song with Chris Difford
1 hr 2 mins across eight videos

How to Sing with Diana de Cabarrus
2 hrs 5 mins across five videos

Ukulele for Beginners with Danny Wootton
2 hrs 55 mins across six videos

Harmonica for Beginners with Ed Hopwood
1 hr 34 mins across twelve videos

Intermediate Harmonica with Ed Hopwood
1 hr 28 mins across thirteen videos

Wellbeing

How to Meditate with Sister Jayanti
1hr 10 mins across three videos

How to Cope with Grief with Julia Samuel
1 hr 3 mins across four videos

How to Live and Eat like an Italian with Kamin Mohammadi
1 hr 38 mins across seven videos

The Happy Kitchen: Good Mood Food with Rachel Kelly and Alice Mackintosh
2 hrs 40 mins across nine videos

A Guide to Modern Manners with Mary Killen
2 hrs 5 mins across four videos

How to Read the Tarot with Daisy Waugh
1 hr 25 mins across eight videos

History

The Seasonal Festivals of Britain with Ronald Hutton
1 hr 50 mins across four videos

A History of London with Dr Matthew Green
6 hrs across six videos

Eminent Victorians with John Mitchinson
2 hrs 3 mins across six videos

A History of British Buildings with Harry Mount
3hrs 20 mins across six videos

An Introduction to the History of Wine with Anne McHale MW
1 hr 17 mins across seven videos

Arts, Crafts and Husbandry

The Idler Guide to Growing Vegetables and Herbs with Alys Fowler
2 hrs 6 mins across four videos

The Idler History of Cooking in Six Chapters with Rowley Leigh
3 hrs 15 mins across six videos

 idler.co.uk/join

OR THE DIGITAL VERSION FOR JUST £69.95

**Worldwide Foraging
with Roger Phillips**

45 mins across five videos

**The Guide to Idle Beekeeping
with Bill Anderson**

3 hrs across seven videos

**How to Make Sourdough
Bread with Bridget Hugo**

2 hrs 16 mins across 23 videos

**How to Cook Ghanaian
with Zoe Adjonyoh**

1 hr 30 mins across six videos

**Release Your Inner Cartoonist
with Harry Venning**

1 hr 10 mins across six videos

**An Introduction to Calligraphy
with Susie Dean**

1 hr 40 mins across nine videos

**Christmas Calligraphy
with Susie Dean**

1 hr 33 mins across seven videos

Work, Business and Technology

**Business for Bohemians
with Tom Hodgkinson**

2 hr 23 mins across ten videos

Public Speaking with David Butter

2 hrs 35 mins across six videos

**Self-Publish Your Book (Beautifully)
with Simon Petherick**

2 hrs 30 mins across nine videos

**The Idler Guide to Negotiation
with Hilary Gallo**

1 hr 30 mins across ten videos

**The Idler Introduction to
Bitcoin with Dominic Frisby**

1 hr 20 mins across eleven videos

**How to Escape with
Robert Wringham**

1 hr 15 mins across six videos

**How to Fix the Future (And Escape
the Grip of Silicon Valley) with
Andrew Keen and Tom Hodgkinson**

I hr 9 mins across ten videos

Classical Studies

**The Idler Guide to Classical
Civilisation with Harry Mount**

1 hr 15 mins across nine videos

**Learn Latin with
Harry Mount Part One**

1 hr 1 min across 13 videos

**Learn Latin with
Harry Mount Part Two**

1 hr across 13 videos

**Learn Latin with
Harry Mount Part Three**

I hr across 11 videos

Fashion

**How to Dress: A Guide for
the Modern Gentleman
with Gustav Temple**

1 hr 55 mins across four videos

 idler.co.uk/online-courses

Idle Pets
Rolex

Owner: Ingrid Sofrin

Rolex is "a bit of a Barbie doll" says Ingrid,
who lives near Penzance in Cornwall

Please send pics of your idle pets to mail@idler.co.uk *or to*
@idlermagazine on Instagram